CW00971460

COMPANY

Revision WorkBook

Andrew McGee MA, BCL (Oxon)

HLT Publications

HLT PUBLICATIONS

200 Greyhound Road, London, W14 9RY

© 1990 The HLT Group Ltd

ISBN 1 85352 762 9

British Library Cataloguing-in-Publication.

A CIP Catalogue record for this book is available from the British Library.

Printed and bound in Great Britain.

CONTENTS

ACKNOWLEDGEMENT

Some questions used are taken or adapted from past University of London LLB (External) Degree examination papers and our thanks are extended to the University of London for their kind permission to use and publish the questions.

Caveat

The answers given are not approved or sanctioned by the University of London and are entirely our responsibility.

They are not intended as 'Model Answers', but rather as Suggested Solutions.

The answers have two fundamental purposes, namely:

a)   To provide a detailed example of a suggested solution to an examination question, and

b)   To assist students with their research into the subject and to further their understanding and appreciation of the subject of Laws.

INTRODUCTION

This Revision WorkBook has been designed specifically for those studying company law to undergraduate level. Its coverage is not confined to any one syllabus, but embraces all the major company law topics to be found in university or polytechnic examinations.

Each chapter contains a brief introduction explaining the scope and overall content of the topic covered in that chapter. There follows, in each case, a list of key points which will assist the student in studying and memorising essential material with which the student should be familiar in order to fully understand the topic. Recent cases and statutes are noted as necessary. However, on the assumption that the student will already possess a textbook/casebook and, for the sake of simplicity, case law has been kept to the bare minimum.

Additionally in each chapter there is a question analysis which looks at past examination questions on similar topics in company papers. The purpose of such a question analysis is to give an appreciation of the potential range of questions possible, and some idea of variations in wording, different formats in questions and alternative modes of combining different issues in one question.

Each chapter will end with at least one, and usually several, typical examination questions, together with skeleton solutions and suggested solutions. Wherever possible, the questions are drawn from University of London external company law papers 1983-89. However it is inevitable that, in compiling a list of questions by topic order rather than chronologically, not only do the same questions crop up over and over again in different guises, but there are gaps where questions have never been set at all. Where a topic or part of one has never been covered in an examination question, a question will have been written as an example, together with skeleton solutin and suggested solution.

Undoubtedly, the main feature of this Revision WorkBook is the inclusion of as many past examination questions as possible. While the use of past questions as a revision aid is certainly not new, it is hoped that the combination of actual past questions from the University of London LLB external course and specially written questions, where there are gaps in examination coverage, will be of assistance to students in achieving a thorough and systematic revision of the subject.

Careful use of the Revision WorkBook should enhance the student's understanding of company law and, hopefully, enable him to deal with as wide a range of subject matter as anyone might find in a company law examination, while at the same time allowing him to practise examination techniques while working through the book.

ABBREVIATIONS

Throughout this Company Law Revision WorkBook the abbreviations CA and IA are used for Companies Act and Insolvency Act respectively. If examination candidates choose to use similar abbreviations when answering examination questions, the full name of the relevant Act should always be given alongside the abbreviated form where it first appears, as in the suggested solutions in this book.

HOW TO STUDY COMPANY LAW

Company law is a subject which is heavily regulated by statute - companies do not exist at common law. Students coming fresh to the subject may therefore get the impression that a knowledge of the statutes is the most important asset for a company lawyer. This is not entirely true. Although the statutes form the basis of the subject, there is also a vast amount of case law, some of which interprets the statutes, while other parts lay down principles which are not to be found in the statutes at all. The subject is one which may also overlap with other areas of law, in particular equity and trusts and contract. There are also occasional criminal liabilities, but it is safe to say that most undergraduate company law courses place relatively little emphasis on these (with the possible exception of insider trading).

Another problem is that the amount of statutory regulation and case law has grown substantially in the past decade, and continues to grow. Because of this it is important for students to look for underlying principles in the subject. If these are grasped, it may well be possible to work out a sensible answer to a problem question even when much of the detailed law has been forgotten. Thus, it is important to know that company law normally operates on a principle of majority rule, that directors are in a fiduciary position in the company, and that the ultimate control rests in the general meeting.

Another important theme running through company law is that of maintaining a balance between the interests of shareholders, creditors and directors. Many apparently complex problems can be reduced to examples of this conflict.

In examinations essay questions tend to fall into two types. One type asks for an account of a particular area of the law. In attempting these questions it is important to identify carefully which area is being asked about and to stick to the point - company law topics are often interwoven, and it is easy to be lured into irrelevancy. It is also necessary to know the material thoroughly. These questions should be avoided by students who are relying on grasp of principle rather than detailed knowledge. The second type of essay question asks about issues of policy, often couched in terms which suggest that the law in a particular area is defective. Obviously, some knowledge of the law is required to answer these questions, but they are also suitable for those with a good grasp of principle.

Problem questions frequently cover a number of different areas. For this reason it is important to look closely at them and to ensure that all the areas are covered. In particular, remember to look at the situation from the point of view of all the parties. Remember that the remedies available to the company are not necessarily the same as those available to the shareholders, and that the directors are separate from the company. Some problems may ask about actions which appear to prejudice the creditors, even though the creditors are not mentioned in the problem: remember to consider their remedies as well.

(A)   REVISION TECHNIQUE

Planning a revision timetable

In planning your revision timetable make sure you don't finish the syllabus too early. You should avoid leaving revision so late that you have to 'cram' - but constant revision of the same topic leads to stagnation.

Plan ahead, however, and try to make your plans increasingly detailed as you approach the examination date.

Allocate enough time for each topic to be studied. But note that it is better to devise a realistic timetable, to which you have a reasonable chance of keeping, rather than a wildly optimistic schedule which you will probably abandon at the first opportunity!

The syllabus and its topics

One of your first tasks when you began your course was to ensure that you thoroughly understood your **syllabus**. Check now to see if you can write down the **topics** it comprises from memory. You will see that the chapters of this WorkBook are each devoted to a syllabus topic. This will help you decide which are the key chapters relative to your revision programme. Though you should allow some time for glancing through the other chapters.

The topic and its key points

Again working from memory, analyse what you consider to be the key points of any topic that you have selected for particular revision. Seeing what you can recall, unaided, will help you to understand and firmly memorise the concepts involved.

Using the WorkBook

Relevant questions are provided for each topic in this book. Naturally, as typical examples of examination questions, they do not normally relate to one topic only. But the questions in each chapter *will* relate to the subject matter of the chapter to a degree. You can choose your method of consulting the questions and solutions, but here are some suggestions (strategies 1-3). Each of them pre-supposes that you have read through the author's notes on key points and question analysis, and any other preliminary matter, at the beginning of the chapter. Once again, you now need to practise working from *memory*, for that is the challenge you are preparing yourself for. As a rule of procedure constantly test yourself once revision starts, both orally and in writing.

Strategy 1

Strategy 1 is planned for the purpose of *quick revision*. First read your chosen question carefully and then jot down in abbreviated notes what you consider to be the main points at issue. Similarly, note the cases and statutes that occur to you as being relevant for citation purposes. Allow yourself sufficient time to cover what you feel to be relevant. Then study the author's *skeleton solution* and skim-read the *suggested solution* to see how they compare with your notes. When comparing consider carefully what the author has included (and concluded) and see whether that agrees with what you have written. Consider the points of variation also. Have you recognised the key issues? How relevant have you been? It is possible, of course, that you have referred to a recent case that *is* relevant, but which had not been reported when the WorkBook was prepared.

Strategy 2

Strategy 2 requires a nucleus of *three hours* in which to practise writing a set of examination answers in a limited time-span.

Select a number of questions (as many as are normally set in your subject in the examination you are studying for), each from a different chapter in the WorkBook, without consulting the solutions. Find a place to write where you will not be disturbed and try to arrange not to be interrupted for three hours. Write your solutions in the time allowed, noting any time needed to make up if you *are* interrupted.

After a rest, compare your answers with the *suggested solutions* in the WorkBook. There will be considerable variation in style, of course, but the bare facts should not be too dissimilar. Evaluate your answer critically. Be 'searching', but develop a positive approach to deciding how you would tackle each question on another occasion.

Strategy 3

You are unlikely to be able to do more than one three hour examination, but occasionally set yourself a single question. Vary the 'time allowed' by imagining it to be one of the questions that you must answer in three hours and allow yourself a limited preparation and writing time. Try one question that you feel to be difficult and an easier question on another occasion, for example.

Mis-use of suggested solutions

Don't try to learn by rote. In particular, don't try to reproduce the *suggested solutions* by heart. Learn to express the basic concepts in your own words.

Keeping up-to-date

Keep up-to-date. While examiners do not require familiarity with changes in the law during the three months prior to the examination, it obviously creates a good impression if you can show you are acquainted with any recent changes. Make a habit of looking through one of the leading journals - *Modern Law Review, Law Quarterly Review* or the *New Law Journal*, for example - and cumulative indices to law reports, such as the *All England Law Reports* or *Weekly Law Reports*, or indeed the daily law reports in *The Times*. The *Law Society's Gazette* and the *Legal Executive Journal* are helpful sources, plus any specialist journal(s) for the subject you are studying.

(B)   EXAMINATION SKILLS

Examiners are human too!

The process of answering an examination question involves a *communication* between you and the person who set it. If you were speaking face to face with the person, you would choose your verbal points and arguments carefully in your reply. When writing, it is all too easy to forget *the human being who is awaiting the reply* and simply write out what one knows in the area of the subject! Bear in mind it is a person whose question you are responding to, throughout your essay. This will help you to avoid being irrelevant or long-winded.

The essay question

Candidates are sometimes tempted to choose to answer essay questions because they 'seem' easier. But the examiner is looking for thoughtful work and will not give good marks for superficial answers.

The essay-type of question may be either purely factual, in asking you to *explain the meaning* of a certain doctrine or principle, or it may ask you to *discuss* a certain proposition, usually derived from a quotation. In either case, the approach to the answer is the same. A clear programme must be devised to give the examiner the meaning or significance of the doctrine, principle or proposition and its origin in common law, equity or statute, and cases which illustrate its application to the branch of law concerned.

The problem question

The problem-type question requires a different approach. You may well be asked to advise a client or merely discuss the problems raised in the question. In either case, the most important factor is to take great care in reading the question. By its nature, the question will be longer than the essay-type question and you will have a number of facts to digest. Time spent in analysing the question may well save time later, when you are endeavouring to impress on the examiner the considerable extent of your basic legal knowledge. The quantity of knowledge is itself a trap and you must always keep within the boundaries of the question in hand. It is very tempting to show the examiner the extent of your knowledge of your subject, but if this is outside the question, it is time lost and no marks earned. It it inevitable that some areas which you have studied and revised will not be the subject of questions, but under no circumstances attempt to adapt a question to a stronger area of knowledge at the expense of relevance.

When you are satisfied that you have grasped the full significance of the problem-type question, set out the fundamental principles involved. You may well be asked to advise one party, but there is no reason why you should not introduce your answer by:

> 'I would advise A on the following matters ...'

and then continue the answer in a normal impersonal form. This is a much better technique than answering the question as an imaginary conversation.

You will then go on to identify the fundamental problem, or problems posed by the question. This should be followed by a consideration of the law which is relevant to the problem. The source of the law, together with the cases which will be of assistance in solving the problem, must then be considered in detail.

Very good problem questions are quite likely to have alternative answers, and in advising A you should be aware that alternative arguments may be available. Each stage of your answer, in this case, will be based on the argument or arguments considered in the previous stage, forming a conditional sequence.

If, however, you only identify one fundamental problem, do not waste time worrying that you cannot think of an alternative - there may very well be only that one answer.

The examiner will then wish to see how you use your legal knowledge to formulate a case and how you apply that formula to the problem which is the subject of the question. It is this positive approach which can make answering a problem question a high mark earner for the student who has fully understood the question and clearly argued his case on the established law.

Examination checklist

1   Read the instructions at the head of the examination carefully. While last-minute changes are unlikely - such as the introduction of a *compulsory question* or *an increase in the number of questions asked* - it has been known to happen.

2   Read the questions carefully. Analyse problem questions - work out what the examiner wants.

3   Plan your answer *before* you start to write. You can divide your time as follows:

   (a)   working out the question (5 per cent of time)

   (b)   working out how to answer the question (5 to 10 per cent of time)

   (c)   writing your answer

Do not overlook (a) and (b)

4   Check that you understand the rubric *before* you start to write. Do not 'discuss', for example, if you are specifically asked to 'compare and contrast'.

5   Answer the correct number of questions. If you fail to answer one out of four questions set you lose 25 per cent of your marks!

Style and structure

Try to be clear and concise. Basically this amounts to using paragraphs to denote the sections of your essay, and writing simple, straightforward sentences as much as possible. The sentence you have just read has 22 words - when a sentence reaches 50 words it becomes difficult for a reader to follow.

Do not be inhibited by the word 'structure' (traditionally defined as giving an essay a beginning, a middle and an end). A good structure will be the natural consequence of setting out your arguments and the supporting evidence in a logical order. Set the scene briefly in your opening paragraph. Provide a clear conclusion in your final paragraph.

TABLE OF CASES

TABLE OF STATUTES

1   CORPORATE PERSONALITY

1.1 Introduction

1.2 Key points

1.3 Recent cases

1.4 Analysis of questions

1.5 Questions

1.1   Introduction

Corporate personality may be defined as the doctrine that a company is for legal purposes an independent person having an existence separate from that of the human beings who own, manage and serve it. For the most part the doctrine is well settled, though there are still some difficulties is working out certain of the implications of the doctrine. These difficulties are considered in the key points section (1.2) below.

1.2   Key points

a)   *Concept of incorporation*

A company is formed by the process of 'incorporation'. This is an administrative procedure, and its correct completion is both necessary and sufficient for the company to exist as an independent legal entity.

b)   *Legal capacity and personality*

Once a company is duly incorporated it has both legal personality and legal capacity.

Legal personality means that the company exists as a legal person. It is distinct from its shareholders, directors and employees. As a separate person it has its own interests, which must be considered separately from those of the humans involved with it.

Legal capacity means that the company can own property and can make contracts in its own name and on its own behalf. In practice this will be done through the agency of human beings, but it is essential to understand that as a matter of law these acts will be the acts of the company.

c)   *Groups of companies*

Particular difficulties arise where there are groups of companies. A company may own some or all of the shares in another company. Where one company has a majority of the shares in another company the first is said to control the second and the two companies form a group. In practice groups of many companies are found.

In principle each company in the group remains a separate legal entity, with its own property and its own rights and liabilities. This principle is sometimes used as a way of minimising or avoiding liabilities, and this may lead to an argument that some or all of the companies in a group should be regarded as a single entity. This is considered further under 'piercing the veil' below.

d) *Piercing the veil*

When a company has been formed it is said to be protected by the 'veil of incorporation'. This means that it is not open to outsiders to argue that the company is really the same person as those controlling it. This is a fundamental principle of company law, but there are exceptions to it. These usually arise where there is evidence that undue advantage is being taken of the principle. The most common exceptions are:

i)   agency: a company may be found to be acting as the agent of its principal shareholders and/or directors, although there is no general presumption that this is so; for an explanation of the principles see *Smith, Stone & Knight* v *Birmingham Corporation* [1939] 4 All ER 116.

ii) fraud: the court may be willing to pierce the corporate veil where it appears that the owners of the company are hiding behind the veil of incorporation for fraudulent purposes. A good example is *Gilford Motor Co Ltd* v *Horne* [1933] Ch 935 where the defendant had entered into a covenant in restraint of trade. He sought to evade it by forming a company to carry on the business which he was prohibited from carrying on. The court held that the existence of the company could be disregarded, so that he was to be treated as being in breach of the covenant.

iii) group enterprises: in *DHN* v *Tower Hamlets* [1976] 3 All ER 462 the Court of Appeal was prepared to pierce the veil of incorporation which would normally have treated members of a group of companies as separate entities. In part this decision may be regarded as having been based on a concept of fraud, but it must also be said that the decision probably goes too far. It is only in the most exceptional cases that companies in a group will be treated as a single entity.

iv) trust: where shares in a company are held on trust, the court may occasionally be prepared to pierce the veil and look at the terms on which they are held - *Abbey Malvern Wells Ltd* v *MLGP* [1951] Ch 728, but it seems that this exception will apply only rarely.

v)   tax: provisions of the taxing statutes sometimes require the piercing of the corporate veil.

1.3   Recent cases and statutes

Insolvency Act 1986 ss212-215. These alter the rules on the personal liability of directors for misconduct in the management of the company's affairs.

Re a Company [1985] BCLC 333: corporate veil can be pierced where there are allegations of fraud.

Winkworth v *Edward Baron Development Co* [1987] 1 All ER 114: alter ego doctrine may provide a way of circumventing corporate personality doctrine.

1.4   Analysis of questions

Corporate personality has been a consistently popular topic, appearing every year since 1983. Five of the questions have been essays, two have been problems. One of the problems (1985 Q6) concerned the rather narrow area of parent-subsidiary relationships, but all the other appearances of this topic have all been straightforward questions on *Salomon* v *Salomon* [1897] AC 22 with only slight variations of emphasis.

1.5   Questions

Type 1:   An essay question on the implications and extent of the corporate personality doctrine.

QUESTION 1

General comment

The four questions listed together below are the four essay questions on corporate personality which have appeared since 1983, and it can readily be seen that all four have the same basic thrust, although the first and last speak of lifting the veil, whilst the other two refer to the concept of legal personality. It may also be noted that the 1984 question is the only one which makes reference to the legislature ignoring the concept of legal personality - all the other questions deal only with the attitudes of the courts.

The following suggested solution will do equally well in answering any of these four questions, except that the passages in square brackets are relevant only to the 1984 question.

'The situations when the courts will lift the veil and disregard the separate legal personality of a company and its members are ill-defined and obscure. It is time that clearer guidelines were established.' Discuss.

University of London LLB Examination
(for External Students) Company Law June 1983 Q1

'Both the courts and the legislature are happy to disregard the principle of the separate personality of the company when it suits them to do so.' Do you agree?

University of London LLB Examination
(for External Students) Company Law June 1984 Q1

'The fact that a company has separate legal personality creates as many problems as it solves and is a fact ignored by the courts at random.' Discuss.

University of London LLB Examination
(for External Students) Company Law June 1986 Q1

'There are no rules, other than the principles of fairness and justice, to dictate when the court should lift the veil of incorporation to attach benefit or detriment to those principally concerned with the company's management.' Discuss.

University of London LLB Examination
(for External Students) Company Law June 1987 Q3

Skeleton solution

Concept of corporate personality - no personal liability - some exceptions - groups of companies - fraud - agency - trusts - taxing statutes - no coherent principle developed.

Suggested solution

The concept of corporate personality, ie the notion that the company is an independent legal person in its own right, separate from its shareholders, was established by the House of Lords in *Salomon* v *Salomon* (1897) where Mr Salomon was allowed to enforce his debentures against the company of which he was also the controlling shareholder. This reversed the view taken in the lower courts, which had held that the incorporation of the business was a sham (Vaughan Williams J) or that there was an agency or trust relationship between Mr Salomon and the company (Court of Appeal). A more modern example of the application of the doctrine is *Lee* v *Lee's Air Farming Ltd* (1961), where the same person was governing director, controlling shareholder and sole employee of the company and the court nevertheless refused to lift the veil. Attention is also drawn to the rule in *Foss* v *Harbottle* (1843), which provides that, subject to very limited exceptions, the proper plaintiff in respect of a breach by the directors of their fiduciary duty to the company is the company itself, even where the wrongdoing has caused loss to individual shareholders.

However, there have been a number of cases where the court has been willing to lift the veil and, [there are also some relevant statutory provisions]. The cases do not lend themselves very readily to a simple and definite classification, but a number of helpful points may be made; for example the veil is more likely to be lifted in cases involving administrative, criminal or revenue law. Four categories of case where it is commonly suggested that the veil will be lifted are fraud or improper conduct, agency, trust and parent-subsidiary relationship. Cases in the first category include *Jones* v *Lipman* (1962) (use of corporate form in an attempt to avoid the effect of a conveyance), *Gilford Motor Co* v *Horne* (1933) (attempt to avoid a restrictive covenant) and *Wallersteiner* v *Moir* (1974) (series of sham companies set up for fraudulent purposes). Cases under the heading of agency include *Gramophone and Typewriter* v *Stanley* (1908), *Smith, Stone & Knight* v *Birmingham Corporation* (1939), *Firestone Tyre* v *Llewellin* (1957). It may be observed in passing that the use of agency is perhaps not properly described as a case of lifting the veil, since, as the House of Lords pointed out in *Salomon* v *Salomon*, there can only be an agency when there are two parties, agent and principal: thus the independent existence of the company is recognised, though its apparent status as principal in the transaction is denied. The third category is rarely found in practice - Lord Denning would have been willing to adopt it in *Littlewoods* v *IRC* (1969) and it was in fact used in the *Abbey Malvern Wells Ltd* (1951) case. The fourth category of case (of which *DHN* v *Tower Hamlets* (1976) is perhaps the best known example) involves a recognition that the subsidiary, though theoretically a separate company, may in fact have very little freedom of manoeuvre: *The Albazero* (1976). Further, it may be a matter of chance whether the parent creates a subsidiary or a branch, and it may be perceived as unfair that this choice should make a fundamental difference to the outcome: *Re Southard & Co Ltd* (1979), per Templeman LJ. There is, however, some evidence to suggest that the courts may be less willing to do this where the subsidiary is not wholly owned: *Multinational Gas and Petroleum Co* v *Multinational Gas Services Ltd* (1983).

In addition to these fairly well-established categories of case there are others of less certain ambit, such as ratification of corporate act (*Cane* v *Jones* (1980)) and determination of residence. Cases such as *Daimler Co Ltd* v *Continental Tyre and Rubber Co Ltd* (1916) and *V/O Sovfracht* v *Udens* (1943), dealing with the alien character of a company, are it is suggested, public policy decisions turning on the existence of exceptional political circumstances; consequently it would be dangerous to draw too general a principle from them. Cases such as *Ebrahimi* v *Westbourne Galleries* (1973), where the court treats the company as a quasi-partnership for the purposes of dealings among the members, may also be regarded as a lifting of the veil, though this example differed from all the others mentioned in that the interests of third parties are not directly involved.

[So far as statute is concerned, the most important examples of lifting the veil are Companies Act 1985 s24 - personal liability if number of members falls below two for more than six months - and Insolvency Act 1986 ss213, 214, dealing with the liability of directors for wrongful trading and directors or members for fraudulent trading.]

It can be seen from the foregoing that the doctrine of corporate personality is not applied very consistently. The courts are prepared to lift the veil (or take some other course having much the same effect) whenever this appears necessary in order to produce a just result. At the same time it must be admitted that corporate personality is taken seriously, and that the veil is not lifted without good reason. It must be considered very doubtful whether legislation could improve the position in an area which calls above all else for judicial discretion.

5

Type 2: A problem question on a particular aspect of corporate personality. This requires careful identification of exactly what is being asked and a proper concentration on those issues to the exclusion of others.

QUESTION 2

Brandy plc is a large public company with a sound and prosperous reputation, as wine suppliers, importers and distributors. Chablis Ltd, and Muscadet Ltd are two of its wholly owned subsidiaries which specialise in the growth and manufacture of particular kinds of wines. The directors of Chablis and Muscadet have always been nominated by Brandy from its own Board of Directors and all profits made by the subsidiaries have been paid directly to the parent company. All decisions by the subsidiaries were required first to be approved by Brandy plc and any overdrafts and other liabilities - such as covenants in leases - were always guaranteed by Brandy. Brandy had also made substantial loans to its subsidiaries, which loans were secured by fixed and floating charges over all the assets of the subsidiaries.

Poor grape harvests in 1982 and 1983 placed the businesses of Chablis and Muscadet in serious jeopardy, but as their connection with Brandy (which itself was actually going through a particularly flourishing period) was well known, creditors continued to extend credit to the subsidiaries. Eventually, however, Chablis and Muscadet were wound up as insolvent, with barely sufficient assets to cover outstanding loan commitments to Brandy.

Advise the liquidator who has been urged by all the creditors, other than Brandy, to do all he can to recover their money.

University of London LLB Examination
(for External Students) Company Law 1985 Q6

General comment

This was a somewhat unusual problem question in that it addressed only the specific area of parent subsidiary relationships. There is a good deal to write about, but candidates should be careful to confine their answers to the points which the question actually raises. The following is suggested as a good attempt at the question.

Skeleton solution

Principle of corporate personality - subject to exceptions - parent-subsidiary is one possible exception - factors relevant in parent-subsidiary cases - element of direction by parent company - policy issue as to piercing the veil in these cases - authorities on both sides - English law has no clear theory on the point - probably no piercing of the veil here.

Suggested solution

In principle these companies must be treated as separate legal entities - *Salomon* v *Salomon* (1897) - but the liquidator will wish to show that this is a case where the veil of incorporation should be lifted so as to treat the companies as a single entity and treat Brandy plc as being liable for the debts of its subsidiaries. Although the *Salomon* v *Salomon* principle is well established, it is also settled that there are a number of exceptions, and the question is whether any of them applies here. *DHN* v *Tower Hamlets* (1976) shows that the parent-subsidiary relationship is one which is potentially susceptible to the lifting of the veil - obviously there are cases where it would be unrealistic to accept separate legal personality for group companies (*Holdsworth* v *Caddies* (1955)). The clearest exposition of the principles in this area was given by Atkinson J in *Smith, Stone & Knight* v *Birmingham Corporation* (1939), when he listed six factors which are relevant in deciding whether to lift the veil on a group of companies. However, the only one of these which is of real relevance to the present case is whether the profits of the subsidiary were made by the parent's skill and direction (compare, for example, *Firestone Co* v *Llewellin* (1956) and *Re FG Films* (1953).) Clearly there is in the present case some element of direction by the parent company.

The difficulty in this case may be summed up by saying that there are two mutually contradictory views of group structure: either may be adopted in any given case, and it is difficult to predict in advance what a court will do. On the side of the formalistic *Salomon* v *Salomon* (1897) analysis it may be argued that the creditors of each company in the group will not necessarily be the same, so that it would be unfair to treat all the companies together (*Charterbridge Corporation* v *Lloyds Bank* (1970)) and this may be so even in the case of a wholly owned subsidiary (*Lonrho* v *Shell* (1980)).

The argument on the other side is that it may be equally unfair to insist too strictly on the doctrine of corporate personality. To quote Templeman LJ in *Re Southard & Co Ltd* (1979), English law allows a parent to spawn a litter of subsidiaries and then strangle the runt, ie to let the weakest of the subsidiaries go to the wall. This may be seen as unfair to creditors of the weak subsidiary and likely to encourage parent companies to engage in unsound speculative ventures through the medium of a subsidiary. A further point made by Templeman LJ in that case is that it is often a matter of chance whether business is conducted through a branch or through a subsidiary, and it would be wrong to allow fundamental consequences to hinge on that choice. Another argument sometimes presented in this context is that groups of companies have to file group accounts and can therefore be treated as a single entity. However, it must be pointed out that these group accounts are in addition to accounts for each individual company, not in substitution for them, a fact which somewhat weakens the force of this argument.

It has been suggested that in cases of this kind it would be desirable to operate a rebuttable presumption that the parent has control of the actions of the subsidiary (in the case of a wholly owned subsidiary this presumption would be conclusive) and a rebuttable presumption that the parent used the subsidiary as an agent. Thus, in cases of this kind the burden of proof would be reversed. It is submitted, however, that this solution would be just as likely to produce unjust results as is that presently adopted. Certainly it would be a very considerable change to the existing position. As things stand at present it must be said that the liquidator's chances of persuading the court to lift the veil are not good. There are some indications of control on the part of Brandy plc, but it is not thought that these are sufficient to warrant lifting the veil of incorporation.

QUESTION 3

Airline Ltd runs a charter flight service to the Channel Islands. The memorandum of association of the company describes the object of the company as 'Air Travel and service to passengers visiting the Channel Islands.' A pressure group called MUD has recently been calling for the company to be subject to tighter regulations, particularly regarding the noise made by its aircraft. They allege that the noise of the aircraft disturbs the wildlife on an important wetland site near the airport. Terry and Martin are the active directors of Airline Ltd. Terry asks his friend Dora to attend the meetings of MUD and attempt to influence the society to withdraw its protest. To this end Dora commissions a report from a scientist promising him £5,000 if the results of his work show that noise is not a factor in disturbing the wildlife. The report was commissioned orally, Dora replying in the affirmative when asked by the scientist; 'I suppose this is on Airline's account?' Terry also entered into a covenant on behalf of the company undertaking to give £10,000 to the group to help in the preservation of wild-life.

In the meantime Martin, who has been attending a trade fair in London, orders two hydroplanes to replace the planes of the company. Each costs £250,000. Martin consulted no-one before placing the order.

1) MUD have withdrawn their objections to the aircraft.

2) The operation of the hydroplanes is uneconomical but the sellers are demanding their price.

3) The scientist is demanding payment from Airline Ltd.

4) MUD are demanding the money covenanted by Terry on behalf of Airline.

Discuss the legal position of the parties.

University of London LLB Examination
(for External Students) Company Law June 1988 Q4

General comment

This is a more typical problem question on corporate personality. The incorporation of an existing business which subsequently declines is similar to the facts in *Salomon* v *Salomon* (1897), and the question invites consideration of three specific areas where the doctrine of corporate personality can have important practical consequences.

Skeleton solution

General principle of corporate personality - some exceptions. Agency possible in insurance policy, but this is contrary to authority. Claim probably fails - Insolvency Act may be available against Jim for wrongful trading: action for fraudulent trading unlikely to succeed - Jim will want veil lifted for compensation purposes - agency possible but unlikely.

Suggested solution

It is a well established principle of company law that a company is an independent legal person, separate from its members and directors - *Salomon* v *Salomon*. The usual consequence of this is that the members of a company are not liable for the debts and other obligations of a company - their liability is limited to the amount which they have agreed to pay for their shares. Conversely, the members cannot in their own name enforce any duties owed to the company.

However, this general principle is subject to exceptions, and three of those exceptions arise for consideration in the present problem. The first issue is whether the liquidator can claim against the insurance company for the loss of business arising from the fire. The difficulty is that the insurance was taken out in Jim's name rather than in that of the company. The situation is therefore similar to that in *Macaura* v *Northern Assurance Co* (1925), where the controlling shareholder was held unable to recover for a loss to the company's timber, since he lacked any insurable interest in it. Although that case may be seen as turning upon a technicality of the law of insurance, the validity of that technicality nevertheless depends upon a finding that the company is a distinct legal person from its controlling shareholder, which is an application of the doctrine of corporate personality. As *Macaura* v *Northern Assurance Co* is a decision of the House of Lords, it is submitted that the liquidator's claim against the insurance company must fail.

The second question is whether the liquidator can make Jim personally liable for any or all of the debts of the company. Again this would be a departure from the *Salomon* v *Salomon* principle, since members' liability is normally limited to the value of their shares, whilst directors as such are not generally liable at all for the company's debts. In this case, though, sections 213 and 214 of the Insolvency Act 1986 are relevant. Section 213 imposes liability in the case of fraudulent trading by a company on anyone who was knowingly a party to such trading; but it seems that this section will only apply where it is possible to establish fraud in the criminal law sense, and this is always difficult. Section 214 imposes liability on a director who has engaged in wrongful trading. This requires only that the director knew or should have known (apparently an objective test) that the company was unable to pay its debts. On the facts stated in the question there appears to be a significant risk that Jim will be held to be guilty of wrongful trading, though the likelihood of a successful action for fraudulent trading is slight.

The third question is whether Jim can claim to be identified with the company for the purpose of claiming compensation from the planning authority. It may be noted that this is one of the rare cases where the controlling shareholder will want the veil of incorporation lifted - there is no element here of protecting third parties. Probably Jim's strongest argument is that the company occupied the premises as agent for him, an approach which succeeded in *Smith, Stone & Knight* v *Birmingham Corporation* (1939) and in *DHN* v *Tower Hamlets* (1976). Strictly speaking this is not a case of lifting the veil, since it recognises the existence of two independent parties (how else could there be an agency relationship?) but the overall result will be what Jim wants. It is difficult to predict what view the court would take, but it is submitted that it would be unduly generous to allow the claim for compensation.

2   THE MEMORANDUM OF ASSOCIATION AND ULTRA VIRES

2.1 Introduction

2.2 Key points

2.3 Recent cases and statutes

2.4 Analysis of questions

2.5 Questions

2.1   Introduction

The doctrine of ultra vires is the doctrine that a company may only lawfully and validly do those things which are included in the objects clause contained in its memorandum of association. Many difficulties arise when companies exceed their objects, and these are examined in this chapter.

2.2   Key points

a)   *The objects clause*

The memorandum of association must state the objects of the company (Companies Act 1985 s2). Originally it was contemplated that companies would be formed for specific limited objects, and that the objects clause was necessary to protect investors in companies from the risk that the company might radically change the nature of its business. In practice objects clauses have grown steadily wider as companies have become aware of the problems caused by an inadvertent ultra vires transaction.

b)   *The objects/powers distinction*

Within the objects clause there may be powers as well as objects. The distinction is that an object is the purpose for which the company is formed, whereas a power is something which can be done as a means of furthering an object, but not for its own sake: *Rolled Steel Products* v *British Steel Corporation* [1982] 3 All ER 1057. Thus, there cannot be an object of borrowing money, though there will normally be a power to do so in order to further the objects of the company. It is important to distinguish between objects and powers, since it is ultra vires to use a power for an improper purpose, whereas it can never be ultra vires to attain an object.

c)   *Implied powers*

In addition to the express powers contained in the memorandum, there is an implied power to do any lawful act reasonably necessary to achieve the objects: *Attorney-General* v *Great Eastern Railway* Co (1880) 5 App Cas 473. Thus, a trading company has an implied power to borrow money. Implied powers cause difficulty because it is inevitably difficult to ascertain in advance their exact ambit. It is likely that this will be established only if the matter goes to court.

d)   *Independent objects*

The distinction between objects and powers is not always welcome to companies, which in many cases want the greatest possible freedom of action. In the late nineteenth century a practice consequently developed of providing in the memorandum that each of the objects was to be construed as an independent object and not subject to any other object. In *Cotman* v *Brougham* [1918] AC 514 the House of Lords upheld the validity of such a clause, but it is to be observed that an independent objects clause does not have the effect of turning powers into objects - it only makes each object independent of each other object.

e)   *The effect of ultra vires transactions*

Generally speaking an ultra vires contract is void: *Ashbury Railway Carriage Co* v *Riche* (1875) LR 7 HL 653. This has important consequences. If the contract is still executory it cannot be enforced by either party. If it has been partly or fully performed, then any payment made or property transferred can be recovered back on the ground of total failure of consideration. Where one party has rendered services under the contract he cannot claim the contract price since the contract is void.

f)   *Companies Act 1985 s35*

The very strict doctrine that an ultra vires contract is void often causes injustice, especially to third parties who have dealt with a company in good faith and then find that they are unable to enforce any contract because it is ultra vires. This position is somewhat mitigated by s35 of the Companies Act 1985, which provides that in favour of a person dealing with the company in good faith any transaction decided upon by the directors is deemed to be free of any limitation of authority contained in the memorandum or elsewhere (ie it is deemed to be intra vires). However, the section has given rise to some difficulties. First, the third party must deal in good faith. This expression is not defined, but is thought to mean that the third party must not in fact be aware of the limitation of authority. Section 35(2) provides that good faith is presumed unless the contrary is proved. The more difficult issue is that the transaction must have been 'decided upon by the directors'. This probably means that a transaction entered into by an employee of the company below director level does not qualify for the protection of s35. In *International Sales and Agencies Ltd* v *Marcus* [1985] 3 All ER 551 it was held that a transaction can fall within this definition when it was authorised by the sole working director, even though the non-executive directors are unaware of it. It seems that the transaction must have been approved by all (or at least a majority) of the directors who commonly participate in the management of the company in order for s35 to apply.

g)   *Corporate gifts and ultra vires*

In a number of cases companies have made or wished to make gifts of various sorts, and it has become necessary to decide whether these were intra vires. The traditional view, laid down in *Hutton v West Cork Railway Co* (1883) 23 Ch D 654, was that all actions had to be taken strictly for the benefit of the company, so that truly charitable gifts were almost bound to be ultra vires. Later cases, such as *Charterbridge Corporation Ltd v Lloyd's Bank Ltd* [1969] 2 All ER 1185 and *Re Horsley & Weight Ltd* [1982] Ch 442, have sought to take a more lenient view, accepting that the making of a gift can sometimes benefit the company in terms of public and/or employee relations. Unfortunately, much of the consideration of these issues has been confused by a failure to distinguish between objects and powers and a disregard of the importance of express objects clauses. Although the position is not altogether clear, it is thought that at the present day a gift authorised by an express objects clause must necessarily be intra vires, whilst in the absence of such a clause it will be necessary to consider whether a power can properly be implied, and this will depend upon finding some object of the company which can legitimately be said to be advanced by the making of the gift.

2.3   Recent cases and statutes

Companies Act 1989 s108 abolishes the doctrine of ultra vires so far as outsiders are concerned, but not for internal company purposes.

International Sales & Agencies Ltd v Marcus [1982] 3 All ER 551: transaction entered into by single active director is 'authorised by the directors' within Companies Act (CA) 1985 s35.

Barclays Bank Ltd v TOSG Trust Fund Ltd [1984] BCLC 1: in interpreting CA 1985 s35 it is not normally necessary to look at the EEC Directive upon which it is based.

Rolled Steel Products Ltd v British Steel Corporation Ltd [1986] Ch 246: considers the distinction between objects and powers in connection with the giving of guarantees.

Brady v Brady (1987) 3 BCC 535: a company cannot give all its assets away. The power to make gifts must be interpreted in the light of the need to give proper protection to creditors.

2.4   Analysis of questions

This has been a consistently popular topic, appearing in the London LLB External examination every year since 1983. On every occasion it has appeared as a problem question, and it has never been paired with any other area of the syllabus, although this could easily be done - liquidations and the rule in *Turquand's case* (1856) being perhaps the most obvious candidates for pairing with ultra vires.

Candidates should be aware that the Companies Act 1989 has made very significant changes in the ultra vires rule; these changes, which are reflected in the answers contained in this chapter may well mean that the importance of this topic (and its appeal to examiners) will be somewhat diminished in the future, though there are of course other matters relating to the memorandum on which questions could still profitably be set. In addition, it should be observed that the 1989 paper included a question on the merits of the (then) proposed change in the law.

2.5 Questions

General comment

All the questions set on this topic in the period 1983-88 have been problem questions on some area of ultra vires activities. Topics which commonly arise are unlawful borrowing and the making of gifts which are not obviously for the benefit of the company. In all these cases the application of s35 of the Companies Act 1985 needs to be considered.

In all the problems which have been set (and in most ultra vires questions which it is possible to imagine) a good answer will begin with a basic recitation of the principle of ultra vires. The following paragraph should therefore be considered as appropriate for the first paragraph of the answer to each of the ultra vires questions set out below. This should be followed by paragraphs dealing with the facts of the particular case, as set out under each of the questions shown.

Suggested solution: introductory paragraph on the principle of ultra vires

The ultra vires doctrine states that a company incorporated under statute (which includes all limited liability companies) derives its objects and powers from its memorandum of association. It can pursue only the objectives stated therein, and possesses only the powers expressly or implicitly conferred upon it, together with such implied powers as are reasonably incidental to the attainment of its authorised objects (*Ashbury Railway Carriage* v *Riche* (1875)). The justification for this rule is said to be that it protects both shareholders and creditors from the consequences of the company's undertaking some other wholly extraneous activity. The validity of this must be considered doubtful in view of the 'independent objects' clause which was accepted by the House of Lords in *Cotman* v *Brougham* (1918). The ease with which a company can alter its memorandum under the present law also deprives creditors of any significant protection. The importance of the doctrine of ultra vires has been further reduced by what is now Companies Act 1985 s35, and the Companies Act 1989 has abolished the doctrine as regards third parties, though not as far as shareholders are concerned. It should be observed that the term ultra vires is sometimes used rather loosely to encompass cases where the directors have exceeded their authority but the act done is not beyond the powers of the company. These are not strictly speaking cases of ultra vires at all, and should properly be dealt with under the rule in *Turquand's case* (1859)*.

*The rule in *Turquand's case* is dealt with in chapter 3.

QUESTION 1

Alan, Bill and Colin are the directors of Alpha Ltd and the articles of association are in the form of Table A of Schedule 1 to the Companies Act 1948. The memorandum of association contains (among others) the following provisions:

'a) The business of the company shall be the construction of houses and all other forms of domestic accommodation.

b) The company may make whatever borrowings and charge whatever of its assets as the directors may consider desirable.

c) The company may make charitable donations.

Each of the above shall be deemed to be an independent main object of the company.'

Although not appointed Managing Director, Alan, to the knowledge and with the full agreement of Bill and Colin (who are both occupied full-time with their own businesses) carries out all that is necessary for the effective operation of Alpha Ltd. Alan recently mentioned to Bill and Colin that he wanted his son (Donald) to join the board and Bill and Colin raised no objection. Alan, acting on behalf of Alpha, agreed that Alpha would make and supply 10,000 school desks for the Dodgem Local Authority and borrowed £100,000 from West Bank plc to enable Alpha to purchase suitable premises and machinery to carry out this agreement. The loan was evidenced by a debenture which was signed on Alpha's behalf by Alan and Donald. Thereafter Donald agreed that Alpha would make a £5,000 contribution to the expenses of Dodgem United, the local football club, for its forthcoming overseas tour and executed a covenant in the name of the company to that effect. Owing to serious mismanagement the company incurred considerable losses and with only 5,000 desks completed was found to be hopelessly insolvent and put into compulsory liquidation.

Advise the liquidator as to the claims being made by West Bank for repayment of the loan and Dodgem United for the agreed contribution to expenses.

University of London LLB Examination
(for External Students) Company Law June 1983 Q6

Suggested solution

After the introductory paragraph above, add the following:

The loan from West Bank: The taking of this loan clearly does not fall within object (a). Clause (b) will, it is submitted, be construed as a power rather than an object, despite *Cotman* v *Brougham* (1918) - it is only in the most exceptional circumstances that a company can have borrowing as an independent object: *Rolled Steel Products* v *BSC* (1986). Consequently it must be concluded that the loan is ultra vires. *Re David Payne & Co Ltd* (1904), which suggests that an ultra vires loan may cease to be ultra vires if the lender is unaware of the ultra vires, must be regarded as incorrect. The question therefore is whether s35 can operate to protect the Bank. The Bank is clearly dealing with the company, and there is no suggestion of bad faith (good faith is presumed - Companies Act (CA) s35(2)). The difficulty is to decide whether this is a transaction decided upon by the directors.

In the case of a single director (and possibly of a managing director who exercises all the powers of the Board) a decision by that individual may be treated as a decision of the directors - *International Sales Ltd* v *Marcus* (1982) - though the ambit of that case is as yet far from clear. In the present case, though, neither Alan nor Donald has been properly appointed, though it might be argued that Alan is a shadow director. It is though unlikely that s35 can render this loan enforceable by the Bank. If s35 does apply, it will be necessary to consider also the problem of Alan's lack of authority. Here it is thought that *Turquand's case* (1856) probably will assist the Bank, since it need not be concerned with the internal arrangements of the company. However, in view of the s35 problems, it is submitted that the liquidator should reject the proof for this claim.

The gift to Dodgem United: The making of charitable donations is here an express object of the company (*Rolled Steel Products Ltd* v *British Steel Corporation Ltd* (1986) confirms that such an object is legally permissible). It is thought that this makes it unnecessary to consider whether this particular donation would benefit the company: *Charterbridge Corporation Ltd* v *Lloyd's Bank Ltd* (1969); *Re Halt Garage Ltd* (1982); *Re Horsley & Weight* (1982). The test propounded by Eve J in *Re Lee Behrens* (1932) may therefore be regarded as inapplicable in the case of an express power. The more difficult point in connection with the present donation is that the decision was taken by Donald, who is not a director. Even if he were a director it appears that a single director has little usual authority: *Rama Corporation* v *Proved Tin* (1952). It is therefore submitted that *Turquand's case* will not help the football club and that the promise of this donation is unenforceable.

QUESTION 2

New School Ltd is a company which is entirely directed by a board of trustees who are the directors of the company. Its objects include:

1)   to educate girls;

2)   to give money to girls to enable them to proceed to higher education;

3)   to do all things the trustees consider desirable.

There is an independent objects clause.

James, Tim and Ron are members of the board of trustees and consequently directors of the company. Ron who is responsible for promoting the good name of the school arranges for the company to donate £20,000 to research into a cure for lung cancer. Without reference to his fellow directors he arranges for the company to create a covenant to this effect. The trustees also authorise a gift to Mary who has been accepted on a course at a finishing school in Switzerland.

Tim and Ron agree with the majority of the directors that boys should be admitted to the school, and five boys are provisionally accepted as pupils at the school, their parents paying deposits of £500 each. One of the parents decides not to send his son to the school and asks for a return of his deposit.

Advise James who objects to the covenant, to pay the £20,000 to the proposed gift to Mary, and to the decision to admit boys. Advise also the parent who wishes to have his deposit returned.

University of London LLB Examination
(for External Students) Company Law June 1984 Q6

Suggested solution

After the standard introductory paragraph add the following:

The covenant: This is ultra vires unless covered by clause (3). The difficulty with giving a literal interpretation to this clause is that it would seem to allow the company to do anything at all, which is contrary to the principle that a company's objects must be limited (*Re Crown Bank* (1890)). The difficulty may be resolved by saying, as in *Bell Houses Ltd* v *City Wall Properties Ltd* (1966), that the clause allows the directors to do anything which they bona fide believe to be in the interests of the company. Even if this is accepted, there is the further difficulty that the decision has been taken by a single trustee. It is, however, unlikely that this will amount to a decision taken by the directors, except where one director is effectively in sole control (*International Sales Ltd* v *Marcus* (1982)) and this does not appear to be the case here.

The gift to Mary: It will no doubt be argued that this is within clause (2). However, there is a problem about the meaning of 'higher education'. It is submitted that a finishing may be further education but is not higher education. On a strict reading, therefore, this gift is ultra vires unless within clause (3), as to which see the discussion above.

The decision to admit boys: This is clearly ultra vires unless covered by clause (3). There does appear to be a majority decision of the trustees to take this course of action, but it is likely that clause (3) will be construed as applying only to things incidental to the achieving of the other objects. Alternatively, the decision might be valid if there were unanimous agreement among the trustees, but that is not the case here. The question then is whether s35 is of any relevance. The parents appear to be dealing with the company, and there is no evidence of bad faith. This transaction appears to have been decided upon by the directors, since there is a majority decision to that effect. It is therefore submitted that the agreement to admit the five boys will be enforceable against the company.

The deposit: In the absence of s35 it is submitted that the deposit can be recovered, since it is money paid under a void (but not illegal) contract. However, s35 requires the lack of vires to be disregarded, and it therefore appears that the contract is fully enforceable.

QUESTION 3

The memorandum of association of Financial Advice plc contains the following clauses:

1)   To provide a publishing service for accountants.

2)   To do all things conducive to the Company's welfare.

3)   To advertise the Company's products.

The memorandum also contained an independent objects clause.

Robin and Betty are two of the directors of Financial Advice plc. When visiting a university to discuss publishing a book on accountancy, Robin is introduced to a physics lecturer and a law lecturer who are both seeking publication of their books. He is impressed by their work and signs a contract with each of them agreeing to publish the books they have written. The contract contains a clause providing that 'Financial Advice plc will advertise the proposed work in all relevant journals'.

When Betty sees the contract, she dislikes the idea of publishing the two books, but after discussing the one proposed book with the law lecturer, she agrees to go ahead. She also agrees that as part of the advance payment, all the recent publications of the company would be given to the college library free of charge.

Betty then places an advertisement for the newly commissioned books in 'Accountants only'.

The chairman of the Board, on hearing of the proposal, has protested vehemently and called on the Board to take no further steps in the production of the book by the lawyer. The Board agrees and also agrees to recover the gift of books to the College library. In the meantime, the physics lecturer has found another publisher whom he prefers and it has become obvious that this book will become an important contribution to science and will sell well.

Discuss.

University of London LLB Examination
(for External Students) Company Law June 1985 Q8

Suggested solution

After the standard introductory paragraph add the following:

The book by the law lecturer does not appear to fall within object (1). It is thought that object (3) is not really an object at all, but merely a power to be used in pursuit of the other objects. Here it is not being so used, and object (3) therefore cannot be relied upon. Object (2) at first sight appears to allow the company to do anything it wants, but this is contrary to the general principle that the company must have limited objects: *Re Crown Bank* (1890). It is likely that this problem will be resolved by saying that the acts done under object (2) must be conducive to achieving the company's main objects, which this does not appear to be. The question therefore is whether the lecturer can rely on s35. He appears to be dealing in good faith, but it is not clear that the transaction was decided upon by the directors. In fact it seems to have been decided upon by only one director. This may be adequate where that director is in effective sole charge of the business (*International Sales Ltd* v *Marcus* (1982)) but the evidence is that this does not apply here. Consequently it is thought that the law lecturer probably cannot enforce the contract.

Similar problems arise in relation to the contract with the physics lecturer. He can rely on the company's lack of capacity if it seeks to enforce the contract against him: *Anglo-Overseas Agencies* v *Green* (1961).

So far as the gift is concerned, it is thought that none of the stated objects clauses will help, since object (2) must, as stated above, be exercised in a way conducive to the good of the company, which requirement is not satisfied here. The company should therefore be able to recover the gift if it has been made already, and need not make it if this has not yet been done.

QUESTION 4

The memorandum of association of Mailorder Plc contains the following clauses:

'The objects of this company are:

a)   To sell goods to the public.

b)   To do all things the directors consider of benefit to the company.

c)   Each of the above objects shall be regarded as a separate and independent object.'

Two of the directors of Mailorder plc become interested in a life insurance scheme. They commission Jack to produce a scheme that will suit the type of people to whom they usually sell goods.   Jack produces the scheme and it is included in the company's next catalogue. The description of the scheme includes a statement that Mailorder Plc has pledged £2,000 to the Royal Society for the Prevention of Accidents.   Jane takes out a policy which (among other things) provides that she must pay premiums for a minimum of two years. Mary is the widow of Fred, whose life was insured under the scheme for £50,000.

Consider the legal position in relation to each of the following matters:

i)   Jack has not been paid.

ii)   Jane has not paid the premium for the second year of her policy, and the company wants the money.

iii)   Mary is seeking payment of £50,000.

iv)   The Royal Society for the Prevention of Accidents ask if theyhave any right to the pledged £2,000.

University of London LLB Examination
(for External Students) Company Law June 1986 Q5

Suggested solution

After the standard introductory paragraph add the following:

The first question is whether the selling of the policies is intra vires. It is not within clause (a) since the policies are choses in action, not goods. On a literal construction it may be within clause (b), but *Re Crown Bank* (1890) shows that clauses of this kind will be restrictively construed as applying only to actions taken to promote the more specific objects of the company - in this sense the decision in *Bell Houses* (1966) must be regarded as having been limited by subsequent authority. The next question is whether s35 of the 1985 Act applies. All the parties seem to be dealing with the company in good faith, but it is unclear whether the transactions have been decided on by the directors. Two directors have agreed; this may be sufficient if there are only three directors, or if the management of the company has been effectively delegated to these two (*International Sales Ltd* v *Marcus* (1982)) but otherwise s35 will not render the scheme intra vires.

Jack may nevertheless argue that there is an implied power to commission independent contractors; this may succeed, but it is submitted that such a power can be used only to further the objects of the company, which is not the case here.

Jane is seeking to avoid the contract rather than to enforce it. *Anglo-Overseas Agencies* v *Green* (1961) shows that the outsider can rely on the company's lack of capacity, and Jane is therefore not obliged to pay further premiums.

Mary is caught in the dilemma over the scope of s35; for the reasons given above it is thought unlikely that her claim will succeed.

So far as ROSPA is concerned, there is no evidence that any pledge was in fact made. If none was made, then clearly the Society has no claim at all. If a pledge was made, the Society's best hope would seem to be to argue that this was intra vires as being made for the good of the company's business under clause (b) as the announcement of the pledge might generate more business for them. This looks tenuous at best. It is unlikely that s35 would help, since the Society does not appear to be dealing with the company - there is no commercial relationship, as required by *International Sales Ltd* v *Marcus*.

QUESTION 5

The Memorandum of Association of Garbage plc includes the following clauses:

1) To recycle waste material

2) To hold property

3) To do all things the directors consider beneficial

4) Clauses (1)-(4) herein constitute separate and independent objects.

Charles, Fred and George are directors of the company. While George is away on holiday Charles and Fred decide to borrow money beyond the limits set out in the articles in order to buy a fleet of barges to carry rubbish from cities out to sea where it would be dumped.

George, while on holiday in Rubelia, is upset by the poverty in the country he is visiting. On his return home he sends £5,000 of the company's money to ease poverty in Rubelia. In the name of the company he contracts to buy 20,000 tons of food from Rubelia, food which that country could otherwise not afford to export and which was rotting in the fields. He believes that the food might be useful for making food flavouring. He also bought, in his own name, a derelict mine which has since turned out to contain rich mineral deposits.

Garbage plc is now in insolvent liquidation. Advise the liquidator.

University of London LLB Examination
(for External Students) Company Law June 1987 Q4

Suggested solution

After the standard introductory paragraph add the following:

The borrowing: A company has a general implied power to borrow in order to pursue its objects: *General Auction Estate & Monetary Co* v *Smith* (1891). Although the borrowing here is beyond the limits set out in the articles, this need not affect the third party - what is in the articles is an internal matter, within the Rule in *Turquand's case* (so that the third party can enforce it unless he had knowledge of the exceeding of authority, as to which there is no indication here), and is not a matter of ultra vires. A more difficult point is whether the loan here is taken to advance the company's objects. Dumping rubbish is not recycling it, and therefore does not fall within clause (1); it may fall within clause (3), but attention is drawn to *Re Crown Bank* (1890), which disapproves of 'anything under the sun' clauses. This clause may, however, be closer to *Bell Houses* (1966), since it is limited to things considered beneficial, and on this basis the action may be intra vires if the directors honestly believe it to be to the benefit of the company.

The gift: There is a general implied power to make gifts where these are for the benefit of the company (*Re Horsley & Weight* (1982)) but it is difficult to see what benefit there is here. The gift is therefore presumably ultra vires, and the recipient will be unable to rely on s35 since there is no evidence of any dealing between the parties.

The food: It is unclear whether this is intra vires. On a liberal construction the making of food flavouring might be considered to amount to recycling waste material, but it is thought that this probably stretches the meaning of the words too much. The supplier will therefore wish to rely on s35, and the difficulty is to decide whether the transaction has been decided upon by the directors. Here only one director has made the decision. *International Sales Ltd* v *Marcus* (1982) shows that this may suffice where that director is in sole effective charge of the company, but this does not appear to be the case here. It is therefore thought that s35 will not aid the supplier.

The mine: The liquidator will naturally wish to claim the benefit of this contract for the company, but it would fairly clearly be ultra vires for the company to enter into the contract - it does not fall within clause (1), and cannot fall within clause (3) since the directors have had no chance to make a decision on whether it is beneficial for the company. In any event George was apparently not acting in his capacity as a director of the company when he made the contract. It is therefore thought that George can keep the benefit of the contract for himself.

QUESTION 6

Airline Ltd runs a charter flight service to the Channel Islands. The memorandum of association of the company describes the object of the company as 'Air Travel and service to passengers visiting the Channel Islands'. A pressure group called MUD has recently been calling for the company to be subject to tighter regulations, particularly regarding the noise made by its aircraft. They allege that the noise of the aircraft disturbs the wildlife on an important wetland site near the airport. Terry and Martin are the active directors of Airline Ltd. Terry asks his friend Dora to attend the meetings of MUD and attempt to influence the society to withdraw its protest. To this end Dora commissions a report from a scientist promising him £5,000 if the results of his work show that noise is not a factor in disturbing the wildlife. The report was commissioned orally, Dora replying in the affirmative when asked by the scientist; 'I suppose this is on Airline's account?' Terry also entered into a covenant on behalf of the company undertaking to give £10,000 to the group to help in the preservation of wild-life.

In the meantime Martin, who has been attending a trade fair in London, orders two hydroplanes to replace the planes of the company. Each costs £250,000. Martin consulted no-one before placing the order.

1)   MUD have withdrawn their objections to the aircraft.

2)   The operation of the hydroplanes is uneconomical but the sellers are demanding their price.

3)   The scientist is demanding payment from Airline Ltd.

4)   MUD are demanding the money covenanted by Terry on behalf of Airline.

Discuss the legal position of the parties.

University of London LLB Examination
(for External Students) Company Law June 1988 Q8

Suggested solution

After the standard introductory paragraph add the following:

Is it intra vires to seek to persuade MUD to withdraw its objections? The answer to this must surely be in the affirmative, since it is reasonably incidental to the main business of the company: *Attorney-General* v *Great Eastern Railway* (1880). More difficulty is caused by the means adopted; the attempt to bribe the scientist is illegal and therefore ultra vires the company. Section 35 will not help the scientist since he can hardly be said to be dealing in good faith if he accepts a bribe; in any event the maxim ex turpi causa non oritur action would seem to preclude his action against the company.

So far as the hydroplanes are concerned the question is whether these come within 'air travel'. It is thought that technically they do not, since hydroplanes operate by gliding across the surface of the water, which is surely sea travel rather than air travel. However, the court may well be prepared to take a more lenient attitude to the construction of the objects clause (for the modern attitude see *Newstead* v *Frost* (1980) and *Rolled Steel Products Ltd* v *British Steel Corporation* (1982)).

The covenant to help in the preservation of wildlife is not within any express object or power and does not seem reasonably incidental to furthering the company's objects, except perhaps on the very tenuous basis that appeasing wildlife groups may help to present future complaints from organisations such as MUD. It is thought, however, that this approach is probably too tenuous to command judicial support and that the covenant will be held to be ultra vires.

3   THE RULE IN ROYAL BRITISH BANK v TURQUAND

3.1 Introduction

3.2 Key points

3.3 Recent cases and statutes

3.4 Analysis of questions

3.5 Questions

3.1   Introduction

The rule in *Royal British Bank* v *Turquand* (1856) is applicable in situations where an officer of the company has exceeded the authority conferred upon him by the company, and the question is whether the company is bound by contracts which he has entered into with third parties.

3.2   Key points

a)   *The basic rule*

In *Royal British Bank* v *Turquand* it was held that an outsider dealing with the company need not be concerned with the internal management of the company, but was entitled to assume that all internal acts had been properly carried out. This is sometimes referred to as the 'indoor management rule'.

The rule does not apply to matters which are contained in the company's public documents (including the memorandum and articles) since the filing of these documents at the Companies Registry operates as constructive notice to all persons of their contents.

Although the major importance of the rule arises in connection with dealings with outsiders, it has been held that a shareholder, or even a director can in appropriate circumstances be treated as coming within the *Turquand* rule: *Hely-Hutchinson* v *Brayhead Ltd* [1968] 1 QB 549.

The application of the rule assumes (and depends upon) good faith in the third party. Thus, an outsider who is in fact aware of the restriction which has been breached cannot rely on the *Turquand* rule: *Rolled Steel Products Ltd* v *British Steel Corporation* [1985] 2 WLR 908.

The *Turquand* rule protects outsiders in respect of internal acts of the company such as proceedings at meetings, but the law of agency remains significant in cases where officers of the company are held out as having authority to enter into particular transactions. The company will be bound only if the contract entered into is one which it is within the actual or apparent authority of the officer to make.

In general a forgery will not bind the company, since it will be a nullity, but in exceptional cases a company which has held the forger out as having authority to execute the document may be estopped from denying its validity: *Ruben* v *Great Finball Consolidated* [1906] AC 439.

b)   *Companies Act 1985 s35*

This section may also serve to help the outsider in enforcing a contract entered into with a company. Where the lack of authority in the company stems from a restriction placed upon the powers of the directors, the contract will be binding in favour of any third party dealing in good faith so long as it was one which was decided upon by the directors. It should be noted, though, that this section is of no help where a more junior official has taken it upon himself to enter into the transaction, since the prohibition will not take the form of a restriction on the powers of the directors and it is unlikely that the transaction will have been decided upon by the directors.

3.3   Recent cases and statutes

Rolled Steel Products Ltd v *British Steel Corporation* [1982] 2 WLR 908: a third party who has knowledge of a relevant restriction on an agent's authority cannot rely on the *Turquand* principle.

3.4   Analysis of questions

This is a topic which, curiously, has not appeared in the London LLB External paper since 1983. Consequently, the questions contained in this chapter are all taken from other sources, and the chapter is included mainly for the benefit of candidates sitting other papers.

Students should be warned that the future of this area of the law is at present very uncertain. It seems likely that the abolition of the ultra vires doctrine will be accompanied by the removal of the constructive notice doctrine, whereby a person dealing with a company is deemed to have knowledge of the contents of the memorandum and articles even though he has not in fact seen them. The amount of space given to the topic here reflects this, and the answers given below also take account of the prospect of legislative change.

3.5   Questions

Type 1:   General essay question

QUESTION 1

'The rule in *Turquand's case* is of no importance in modern company law.' Discuss.

Written by Editor
September 1989

General comment

This is a very standard essay question on this topic. The approach adopted must necessarily be heavily conditioned by the changes made in the Companies Act 1989.

Skeleton solution

Rule allows outsider to ignore the indoor management of the company - does not apply to ultra vires transactions - outsider must act in good faith - rule seems to be wider than ordinary agency, though this is disputed - rule is available only to outsiders and does not apply to forgeries - statutory rules on ultra vires (CA 1985 s35 and CA 1989 s108) restrict the rule still further, but it continues to have some significance.

Suggested solution

The rule in *Turquand's case* may be stated as being that an outsider, dealing with the company in good faith, is not required to investigate any limitations on the authority of any official of the company to enter into transactions on the company's behalf. Two important aspects of this rule must immediately be noted. The first is that it does not apply to transactions which are ultra vires the company. The rule is concerned only with the internal management of the company. The memorandum and articles are public documents, and any restriction contained therein on the power of the company to enter into transactions is deemed to be known to all those who deal with the company, irrespective of the true position (subject to the impact of Companies Act (CA) 1985 s35, which is considered below). The second point is to stress the requirement of good faith on the part of the outsider. This has been held to mean that the outsider is protected only when the employee or officer of the company is acting within his apparent authority: *Hely-Hutchinson* v *Brayhead* (1968). When viewed in this light the issue appears to be merely an application of the ordinary rules of agency, on the basis that the employee or officer is an agent of the company and will bind the company by any intra vires act so long as it falls within his actual or apparent authority. It has been argued, however, that this is a misunderstanding of the rule, which depends purely on considerations of commercial convenience, and it must be admitted that the rule has not traditionally been seen as being part of the doctrine of agency. A further point in connection with the good faith requirement is that the outsider must not have been put upon enquiry by any circumstance known to him as to whether the internal management requirements have been properly complied with: *Rolled Steel Products Ltd* v *British Steel Corporation* (1986).

Another important aspect of the rule is that it protects only outsiders - insiders within the company cannot rely upon it: *Howard* v *Patent Ivory Manufacturing Co* (1888), *Morris* v *Kanssen* (1946).

So far as documents are concerned, the doctrine applies only to genuine documents and not to forgeries: *Kreditbank Cassel* v *Schenkers* (1927).

As mentioned above, CA 1985 s35 has some impact on the *Turquand* rule, since it applies to all limitations on the authority of the directors, not just those contained in the memorandum and articles. This section allows a third party, dealing in good faith with the company, to ignore any such restrictions, and this is more liberal towards the outsider than is the *Turquand* rule, since good faith is presumed unless the contrary is proved. It is important, however, to notice the limits of this principle. It applies only to transactions decided upon by the directors, whereas the *Turquand* rule applies to any acts of the company. The widening of s35 in the 1989 Companies Act will be of some further help to outsiders, but will not of itself remove the problems in this area.

The changes to the constructive notice rule provide greater protection for outsiders, since the requirement of good faith (in the sense of not having knowledge of any limitation) has been removed. Consequently it will less often be necessary to rely on the traditional agency notions implicit in the *Turquand* rule. Nevertheless, the rule continues to be of some importance in company law, and will probably do so for some time to come.

Type 2: Problem question

QUESTION 2

Large plc was the beneficial owner of all the issued share capital of two companies, Small Ltd and Medium Ltd.

Tiny was known as the 'group finance director of the Large plc group of companies', although he had not been appointed a director of any of the companies; he conducted the financial negotiations on behalf of all companies in this group with the Left Bank. Tiny decided that the business of the group was being hampered by transportation problems and that Medium Ltd should purchase a new fleet of vehicles. The Left Bank agreed to provide the finance, but required Small Ltd to guarantee the indebtedness of Medium Ltd. So Tiny signed the bank's form of guarantee 'for and on behalf of Small Ltd' and the loan was made.

Medium is now in insolvent liquidation. Discuss the rights of the Left Bank in respect of the loan.

Written by Editor
September 1989

General comment

A standard problem question raising the issues of extent of actual and apparent authority.

Skeleton solution

Central issue is Tiny's authority - lack of formal appointment not decisive - Tiny is probably Small's agent - alternatively he may be personally liable - CA 1985 s35 not relevant - Large probably not liable.

Suggested solution

The principal issue here is whether Medium Ltd (or indeed any other companies in the group) can be held liable for Tiny's activities. Tiny had never formally been appointed a director, but he had been invested with de facto authority to deal with the group's financial matters, and it seems likely that the Bank (and no doubt others) dealt with him on this basis. It is possible to discover who is a director by examining the company's public documents at Companies House, though in practice this is very rarely done. As Medium Ltd is in insolvent liquidation the bank will want to take action against Small Ltd as guarantor. The giving of such guarantees is unlikely to be ultra vires Small Ltd, so that the only problem appears to be Tiny's lack of authority. It is submitted that Tiny is to be regarded as Small Ltd's agent for this purpose, having been held out as such by the company when it let him handle the financial matters for the group generally. It therefore appears that, either on the basis of agency, or on the basis of the rule in *Turquand*, the bank can enforce the guarantee given by Tiny on behalf of Small Ltd. The company may then be able to take action against Tiny personally if he has in fact exceeded his authority by giving the guarantee.

If it were necessary to rely on Companies Act 1985 s35, it is thought that this would not help the bank. The transaction here was not decided upon by the directors, so that the section would have no application.

The conclusion therefore is that the loan is recoverable from Medium Ltd, to the extent that the company has assets available, or against Small Ltd on the basis of the guarantee. There appears to be no chance of recovering anything from Large plc, since that company was not a party to any of the relevant transactions.

QUESTION 3

The articles of association of Codge Ltd authorised the appointment of a Managing Director, who was to be entitled to exercise all the powers of the Board. The company's affairs are conducted in a very lax manner, and Smith has taken upon himself the performance of the duties of Managing Director, although no formal appointment to that position has ever been made. The other directors have no knowledge of Smith's activities, largely because they do not concern themselves with the day-to-day running of the company. Smith commissions Donald to install a new heating system in the company's factory. The work is carried out satisfactorily, but the company refuses to pay for it. Advise Donald.

Written by Editor
September 1989

General comment

This is another question dealing with the difficulties which arise when a person's de facto authority exceeds that which has been formally conferred upon him. In an examination context it seems likely that this would appear as a part of a question, since there is not enough material in it to make a full question.

Suggested solution

It is clear that the commissioning of the heating system is not likely to be ultra vires the company. The only difficulty which arises is whether Smith had the authority to bind the company to the contract. We are told that he has not been appointed director, but that he acts in that capacity. This is similar to the case of *Hely-Hutchinson* v *Brayhead* (1968), where the de facto managing director entered into contracts on the company's behalf, and it was held that the company was bound by those contracts.

The only possible ways of avoiding this conclusion would be if Donald were not an outsider to the company (*Morris* v *Kanssen* (1946)), or if he knew of Smith's lack of authority and was therefore not dealing in good faith when he took on the contract (*Rolled Steel Products* v *British Steel Ltd* (1985).

4   THE ARTICLES OF ASSOCIATION

4.1 Introduction

4.2 Key points

4.3 Recent cases and statutes

4.4 Analysis of questions

4.5 Questions

4.1   Introduction

This chapter deals with the problems arising from the provisions contained in a company's articles of association, and in particular from the concept that these articles form a contract involving the members and the company.

4.2   Key points

a)   *Companies Act 1985 s14*

This section provides that the articles of association are a contract binding as if they had been signed and sealed by every member of the company. In *Wood* v *Odessa Waterworks* (1889) 42 Ch D 636 it was held that this provision must be read as if it also deemed the company to have signed and sealed the articles. The contract is multi-partite, invloving the members inter se and each member individually with the company.

The s14 contract may be enforced by any member of the company, but there is some uncertainty as to the rights which may be enforced by means of s14. One view is that s14 may only be used in connection with what are sometimes termed 'membership rights' ie those rights whose violation will affect the member in his capacity as a member. However, it is suggested that the better view is that the rights of the member include the right to have the company's affairs managed in accordance with any provisions in the articles, irrespective of theoretical debates about the nature of membership rights.

The narrower view of the s14 contract rests on the decision of Astbury J in *Hickman* v *Kent & Romney Marsh Sheepbreeders' Association* [1915] 1 Ch 881, whilst the broader view appears in *Salmon* v *Quin & Axtens* [1909] AC 442.

Case law suggests that there are certain respects in which the s14 contract differs from an ordinary contract. Thus, it is not subject to rectification, even where it appears that the normal requirements for this remedy are fulfilled: *Scott* v *Frank Scott (London) Ltd* [1940] Ch 794. Nor can damages be awarded against the company for a breach of the contract, since this would be a misuse of the company's funds: *Houldsworth* v *City of Glasgow Bank* (1880) 5 App Cas 317.

In *Eley* v *Positive Government Security Life Assurance Co* (1876) 1 Ex D 88 it was held that the s14 contract could not be used to enforce the right to be company secretary, even where this right was contained in the articles, but this decision must be regarded as being of doubtful authority at the present day, especially if the wider view of s14 is to be adopted.

b)   *Altering the articles*

CA 1985 s9 permits the alteration of the articles by Special Resolution. Difficulties sometimes arise where it is alleged that the majority has made an alteration for the purpose of treating the minority unfairly. *Allen* v *Gold Reefs of West Africa* [1900] 1 Ch 656 establishes that the power to alter the Articles must be exercised bona fide in the best interests of the company. Those seeking to overturn an alteration face a heavy burden of proof, but may be able to succeed if they can prove either that the majority are acting from a wrongful motive, so that they are not bona fide, or that the proposed change discriminates unfairly between different shareholders, so that it is not truly in the best interests of the company. This is an area where there is room for a considerable amount of judicial discretion, and it is very difficult to predict in advance what view a court will take of a particular case.

4.3   Recent cases and statutes

Mutual Life Insurance Co v *The Rank Organisation* [1985] BCLC 11: the court will not imply into the articles of association a clause conferring equal pre-emption rights on all shareholders.

4.4   Analysis of questions

This topic has appeared three times since 1983, twice as a problem and once as an essay. A number of other questions have consequently been included. It is considered that this topic has considerable potential for the future, and that the questions set on it in recent years have by no means exhausted the range of possible questions.

This topic can very readily be paired with that of the memorandum of association (as in Question 1 below), but generally tends to appear by itself.

4.5   Questions

Type 1: Essay question

QUESTION 1

'Although it is clearly established that the memorandum and articles of association constitute a contract between the company and its members, it is a contract which deviates significantly from an orthodox contract.' Discuss.

University of London LLB Examination
(for External Students) Company Law June 1988 Q1

General comment

This question is effectively an invitation to discuss the contents of the contract in the memo and articles and to comment on its unusual features.

Skeleton solution

The s14 contract has certain special features - these tend to restrict its value - no rectification, no damages for breach - contract can be altered in accordance with the statutory procedures - usual view is that contract can only be used to enforce membership rights, but this is subject to academic dispute.

Suggested solution

Section 14 of the Companies Act 1985 provides that the memorandum and articles shall have effect as if they were contained in a contract signed and sealed by every member of the company and containing covenants on the part of each member to obey them. These words are not on the face of them sufficient to make the company a party to the contract, but it was held in *Wood* v *Odessa Waterworks Co* (1889) that they do have that effect. The explanation of this is apparently that the draftsman of the original legislation had not appreciated that companies were to have legal personality.

Although this is a notional contract, the court has no jurisdiction to rectify the Articles, even if they do not represent the common intention of the original members: *Scott* v *Frank Scott (London) Ltd* (1940).

If the contract is broken, the remedies are limited to declaration and injunction. Damages cannot be awarded, for the capital of the company may only properly be used to attain the objects of the company: *Houldsworth* v *City of Glasgow Bank* (1880).

The s14 contract is naturally subject to the provisions of the companies legislation, and therefore cannot be used to sidestep those provisions. One relevant provision in those Acts is that the memorandum and articles can be altered by certain specified procedures. A duly effected alteration will amount to a valid variation of the terms of the contract even in the case of a member who voted against the change.

The extent of the contractual rights and obligations has also been considered in the decided cases, and a somewhat restrictive view has been taken. The leading case is *Hickman* v *Kent & Romney Marsh Sheep-breeders' Association* (1915), where it was said that the rights protected by the section are only those which members have in their capacity as members. Thus a member can sue to be allowed to vote at meetings - *Pender* v *Lushington* (1877) - or to recover a dividend - *Wood* v *Odessa Waterworks* - but not to be company secretary, even where this right is enshrined in the articles: *Eley* v *Positive Government Security Life Assurance Co* (1876).

The s14 contract can also be enforced by members inter se: *Rayfield* v *Hands* (1960).

It may be mentioned in passing that the traditional view of the s14 contract has been challenged, not least by Wedderburn, and there are cases, such as *Salmon* v *Quin & Axtens* (1909), which seem to run counter to the traditional view. The alternative theory is that every member has a right to have the company's business conducted in accordance with the articles, but this seems to be a minority view at the present day.

There is some evidence that before the decision in *Hickman* both views had strong supporters. If so, then that decision must, it is submitted, be regarded as having decided the issue in favour of the narrower view of the s14 contract.

Type 2: Problem questions

One problem question appears below. Two further problem questions (1983 Q8 and 1987 Q6) also involve other issues, and are therefore considered in chapter 13: *Minorities* (Question 1) and chapter 12: *Directors* (Question 2) respectively, where the points relating to the articles of association are also covered.

QUESTION 2

Quill Ltd, a private company with issued share capital of £80,000 is in need of additional working capital. Penn, an outsider to the company, is prepared to invest £20,000 on the following terms:

(1) that he will be a director of the company as long as he wishes to remain one.

(2) that he will have a veto over all decisions of the board of directors.

(3) that if the company is successful he will have the right to acquire a controlling interest in the company, but in the meantime he is to receive a guaranteed 18% return on his investment in the company.

Consider to what extent Penn's wishes can be effectuated, and advise him as to the best way to safeguard his interests.

Written by Editor
September 1989

General comment

It should be noted that this question is not restricted to the articles of association, since there may be ways of safeguarding Penn's interests which do not rely on the articles. However, the answer given here will concentrate on solutions involving the articles.

Skeleton solution

Choose between equity and debt - *Bushell* v *Faith* clause needed to protect position as director, with adequate weighting - veto over board decisions should be put in the articles - guaranteed return to be achieved by preference shares.

Suggested solution

Penn wishes to invest £20,000. If he invests this solely as share capital, he will have 20% of the shares, which will not even allow him to block a Special Resolution. As share capital is risk capital there is the further point that he could lose the whole of his investment. An alternative would be for him to invest some or all of the money in the form of a loan. This carries somewhat less risk of loss, since the loan would presumably be secured by a charge on the company's assets, but if he is not a shareholder he cannot be given voting or other membership rights. This needs to be borne in mind when considering the best scheme.

His first wish is to remain a director as long as he wishes. The difficulty here is that Companies Act 1985 s303 provides that a director can always be removed by Ordinary Resolution of the company, notwithstanding any contrary provision in the articles. The solution to this dilemma is found in the case of *Bushell* v *Faith* (1970), where the House of Lords upheld the validity of a clause giving a director weighted voting rights on any resolution to remove him from office, notwithstanding that the effect of this was to render him immune to removal. Clauses of this kind are now commonplace in small private companies. It will be necessary to give Penn enough weighting to ensure that he can by himself defeat any such resolution. Thus, if he is to have 20% of the shares he should be given five votes per share. Indeed, it may be preferable to give him rather more than five votes, since there can be no guarantee that his shareholding will not be diluted in future years. Twenty votes per share should be enough to keep him safe for the foreseeable future. The granting of these weighted voting rights will of course require a change in the articles, and Penn should insist on the making of this change as a condition of his buying the shares. The clause must be carefully drafted so that the weighted voting rights apply also to any attempt to remove that clause from the articles at a future date.

Penn's second wish to is to have a veto over all decisions of the board of directors. Again, a clause can be inserted into the articles to this effect, entrenched in the same way as the *Bushell* v *Faith* clause alluded to above. such a clause appears to be enforceable against the other directors; in *Salmon* v *Quin & Axtens* (1909) a right of veto was upheld, but this case has been criticised for allowing rights other than membership rights to be enforced by means of the s14 contract. It is nevertheless submitted that the case is correctly decided, since the rights of a member include the right to have the affairs of the company conducted in accordance with the articles. An alternative approach for Penn would be to enter into a contract with the company, independently of the articles, which would give him this right of veto.

Penn's third wish is to have a guaranteed return of 18%, together with a right to take control if the company is successful. This is much more difficult to achieve. So far as a guaranteed rate of return is concerned, there appear to be two approaches. The simplest is for Penn to grant a loan secured by debenture at 18% interest. However, this will prevent him from buying shares (unless he puts in more than the £20,000) and the schemes proposed above for his first two requirements depend on his being a shareholder. The other approach is to give him preference shares, carrying a dividend of 18%. This works so long as the company has profits out of which to pay the preference dividend, but not otherwise, and is for that reason less safe than the debenture. Care will also be needed in relation to the voting rights attached to the preference shares, so as to ensure the meeting of the other two requirements. It would be possible to draft the articles so that any decision of the board of directors is subject to veto by the preference shareholder (ie Penn) but this will not work for the question of removal from office. Instead, the preference shareholder will have to be allowed to vote on this matter, and to have the weighted voting rights discussed above.

As to taking control of the company, it seems that Penn requires some form of option to buy at least some of the remaining shares, exercisable within a specified (but fairly lengthy) time. No attempt should be made to define the concept of the company being 'successful' - from Penn's point of view he can decide for himself whether it is successful enough that he wants to buy it. It would not be appropriate to include the option in the articles, not least because it is a contract between Penn and the other shareholders, to which the company is not a party. So long as he gives proper consideration for the option there should be no difficulty about its enforceability.

5   PROMOTERS AND PRE-INCORPORATION CONTRACTS

5.1 Introduction

5.2 Key points

5.3 Recent cases and statutes

5.4 Analysis of questions

5.5 Questions

5.1   Introduction

The title of this chapter really encompasses two separate areas of law. The first concerns the liability of promoters for statements contained in a company prospectus issued prior to a flotation, whilst the second concerns the extent to which the company can be made liable, after incorporation, for contracts entered into, purportedly on its behalf, prior to incorporation. The two areas are covered in the same chapter because they both relate to the very early stages of a company's existence and consequently often occur together in a problem question.

5.2   Key points

a) *Prospectuses*

Only a public company may issue a prospectus. Private companies are forbidden to offer their shares to the public.

The contents of the prospectus are tightly regulated by the Financial Services Act 1986 (replacing the Prevention of Frauds (Investments) Act 1958).

It is an offence under the Companies Act 1985 to announce the issue of a prospectus containing an untrue statement.

Section 19 of the Theft Act 1968 makes it an offence to conspire with others to defraud the company, and this offence may be committed where a misleading prospectus is issued.

b) *Promoters*

There is no statutory defintion of the term 'promoter', but it is generally understood to mean those who take on the task of forming the company and getting it underway in its business.

Promoters owe fidcuiary duties to the company, although they cannot be treated as its agents during the period of promotion, for the company does not exist at that time. In particular they must not make a secret profit out of the process of formation. This is of particular importance if the promoters are intending to sell their own property to the company. Full disclosure of the circumstances must be made, either to the shareholders or to an independent board of directors. In many cases there will be no independent board, since it is likely that the promoters themselves will become the directors.

Promoters have a duty to account to the company for the profits of any property which they have bought for the purpose of selling it to the company. In equity the property belongs to the company, which is therefore entitled to insist on taking it over at cost price.

Promoters have a duty not to exercise undue influence over the decisions of the company.

Where promoters are in breach of their duties the company will be able to sue for any damages incurred, or claim an account of any profits made. If a contract has been improperly procured, then it is likely that the company will be able to rescind it.

In this area many of the remedies depend upon general contractual and tortious principles (including the tort of deceit). In any case it is necessary to consider the application of these principles.

c)   *Pre-incorporation contracts*

When a company is in the process of formation it is common for contracts to be entered into on its behalf. This is a logical impossibility, since by definition the company does not exist at that point. After incorporation it may become necessary to consider who, if anyone, is liable on the contract.

CA 1985 s36(4) provides that a person who enters into a contract as purported agent for an unformed company is deemed to have made the contract in a personal capacity and is personally liable on it. This rule is subject to contrary agreement between the parties to the contract, but it is impotrtant to understand that the contrary agreement cannot serve to make the company liable on the contract.

The only way in which the company can become liable is if, after incorporation, it enters into a contract with the original creditor in the same terms as that of the orginal contract between the promoter and the creditor. It is not possible simply to ratify the original contract, since the principles of agency do not permit ratification of a contract made when the purported principal did not exist.

5.3   Recent cases and statutes

The Financial Services Act 1986 significantly amends the rules relating to the contents of prospectusses and liability for misstatements therein.

5.4   Analysis of questions

This is a topic which has occurred on the London LLB External paper six times since 1983, and which is popular in degree examinations more generally. It is therefore given extensive treatment in this book. On the London paper it has always appeared as a problem question, though there is no obvious reason why it cannot be set as an essay question - suitable essay answers are to be found at the end of this chapter.

5.5   Questions

Type 1: Problem questions, usually encompassing both duties of promoters and liability for pre-incorporation contracts

QUESTION 1

In 1982 Percy, Quentin and Ronald formed a syndicate to purchase from Victor an exclusive licence to sell in the United Kingdom electrical goods manufactured by a Japanese company. They agreed to pay Victor £500,000 for the licence and also purchased for £50,000 the right to certain debts of £80,000 owed to Victor.

They decided to form a public company (Perquero plc), sell the licence to the company and invite the public to subscribe for a minority of the share capital. The money so raised would be used to pay Victor. The registration documents were sent to the Registrar of Companies on January 3rd 1983 but, because of a postal delay, did not reach him until January 14th. On January 15th on notepaper headed 'Perquero plc', Percy ordered goods from Sam. The letter concluded, 'Yours faithfully, Perquero plc', and Percy appended his own signature underneath. Sam supplied the goods but has never received payment for them. The Registrar issued a certificate of incorporation to Perquero plc on January 20th.

In March 1983 Perquero plc obtained the agreement of the Stock Exchange to the listing of forty per cent of its ordinary share capital and it issued a prospectus signed by Percy, Quentin and Ronald as directors inviting subscriptions for the shares at £2 each. The prospectus gave details of the purchase of the licence, but did not disclose that Percy, Quentin and Ronald purchased the debts owed to Victor. In addition it did not disclose that the licence was terminable by the Japanese company on a month's notice, as Percy, Quentin and Ronald believed this eventuality most unlikely and stated that the business was certain to grow and prosper. Albert purchased 100 shares on the faith of the prospectus.

In April, Percy, Quentin and Ronald enfored the repayment of the debts and recovered £75,000. The Japanese company terminated the licence and Perquero plc's business collapsed. Albert sold his shares at 50p each before dealings were suspended with the shares in Perquero plc listed at 10p each. In May Perquero plc went into liquidation.

Discuss.

University of London LLB Examination
(for External Students) Company Law June 1983 Q4

General comment

A fairly typical question, involving both aspects of this topic.

Skeleton solution

Definition of 'promoters' - position of co-promoters - duty of promoters not to make a secret profit - requirement of honest disclosure of profit - deficiencies in prospectus - civil and criminal penalties - Albert's common law remedies - possible Insider Trading - pre-incorporation contract not enforceable against company - agent's personal liability, CA 1985 s36.

Suggested solution

The persons who undertake to form a company and set it in operation, and who take the necessary steps for that purpose are known as 'promoters' (*Twycross* v *Grant* (1877), per Cockburn CJ). The Companies Act gives a very wide definition of 'promoter', encompassing all those connected with the formation of a company except those who provide only professional advice in that connection (eg lawyers, accountants).

Whether co-promoters are partners for this purpose depends upon the circumstances (ie it is a question of fact, as is the determination of a partnership in all other cases: *Keith Spicer* v *Mansell* (1961)). If they are partners, then they are jointly and severally liable for each others' defaults. If they are not partners, then the liability is purely several in the absence of contrary agreement: *Hamilton* v *Smith* (1859).

A promoter is not allowed to make a secret profit from the promotion of the company: *Re Cape Breton* (1885). If any profit is to be made, there must be full and honest disclosure to all members of the company: *Lagunas Nitrate Co* v *Lagunas Syndicate Ltd* (1889). 'Honest' disclosure means that it is not enough to make disclosure to cronies who are the present members when it is intended to use partial disclosure to induce others to join later.

Turning first to the prospectus, it can be seen that it is deficient in a number of respects. It fails to mention the purchase of debts (a secret profit for the promoters); nor does it state that the licence can be terminated. There are civil and criminal penalties for defective prospectuses. It is an offence under the Companies Act to announce the issue of a prospectus containing an untrue statement. Also relevant is s19 of the Theft Act 1968, which makes it an offence for an officer of the company with intent to deceive the company's members to publish or concur in publishing a written statment which may be misleading in a material particular. This offence may well have been committed here. Section 160 of the Financial Services Act (replacing Prevention of Fraud (Investments) Act 1958) may also be relevant.

Albert has bought shares on the faith of the defective prospectus and may also have remedies at common law. He may be able to sue the promoters for deceit, though this requires proof of fraud, which is always difficult: see, for example, *Derry* v *Peek* (1889), *Edgington* v *Fitzmaurice* (1885). Negligent misrepresentation under *Hedley Byrne* v *Heller* (1963) is another possibility, but it would be easier and simpler for Albert to rely on the statutory right to claim compensation from the promoters given to anyone who is induced to take shares or debentures by an untrue statement in the prospectus.

However, a word of warning to Albert is also appropriate. His sale of the shares just before the supension looks suspicious. If he acted on inside information, then he may well have committed an offence under the Company Securities (Insider Dealing) Act 1985.

A further problem arises because goods were ordered before the company had come into legal existence by being formed. The company is not bound by this contract, since it did not exist when the contract was made, and it appears that the law will not permit the company to ratify the contract after formation. The only way in which the company can be bound is if a new contract is entered into: *Melhado* v *Porto Alegre Railway Co* (1874).

Though the company is not liable, the promoters may be. Companies Act 1985 s36 provides that a promoter is liable in these circumstances unless there is contrary agreement, of which there is no mention here. It is therefore concluded that Percy will be personally liable on the contract, the old distinctions turning on the capacity in which the promoter signed having been abolished by s36: *Phonogram* v *Lane* (1982).

QUESTION 2

James, Harry and Francis wish to further the restoration of steam railways. In pursuance of this aim James buys three miles of disused railway track from British Rail for £400. Meanwhile Harry is involved in the formalities of forming a company to further the work of restoring steam railways. Francis orders two steam engines and tools and materials to restore them from a firm known as Junk Bros. He tells them that the company which Harry is forming will take over the contract to buy, transport and restore the engines. Harry completes the formalities and the company is formed. James sells the land to the company for £1,000 and the company resolves to take over the liabilities of Francis and pay Harry the expenses involved in promoting the company.

The company formed by James, Harry and Francis then decides to raise capital by becoming a public company quoted on the stock exchange. It issues a prospectus in which it names only Harry and Francis as promoters and describes the acquisition of the land for £1,000 but gives no further details. The company has failed and is in liquidation.

Discuss.

University of London LLB Examination
(for External Students) Company Law June 1984 Q5

General comment

This question also involves both aspects of this topic, but the suggested answer illustrates another important point for which students must watch out. Where the question asks students to advise investors or promoters, or simply calls for discussion of the problem, it is important to examine at some length the ways in which promoters may be criminally liable and the ways in which they may have civil liability to investors. By contrast, where, as in the next question, students are asked to advise the liquidator, these matters are of relatively little importance, since the liquidator's duty is to increase the assets of the company as far as possible for distribution to creditors, and the liability imposed on promoters is not a liability to the company and will therefore not help the liquidator in this task.

Skeleton solution

Definition of promoters - promoter liable on pre-incorporation contract in the absence of contrary provision - company not liable - H's expenses likely to be dealt with in articles - prospectus deficient in disclosing facts - duty of promoter not to make secret profit - possible criminal liabiliy no help to liquidator - promoters may incur civil liability to investors.

Suggested solution

The liquidator here has essentially two problems. The first concerns the validity of pre-incorporation contracts, whilst the second relates to defective prospectuses.

James, Harry and Francis are clearly within the definition of 'promoters' given by Cockburn CJ in *Twycross* v *Grant* (1877) - 'A person who undertakes to form a company with reference to a given project, and to set it going and ... takes the necessary steps to accomplish that purpose.' Where promoters of a company make a contract, purportedly on behalf of that company, at a time when the company has not yet been formed, the question arises whether the company is bound by the contract once it comes into existence. In the case of the contract with Junk Bros the liquidator will want to know whether the company is liable or whether Francis should be pursued as a personal contracting party. Before the enactment of s9 of the European Communities Act 1972 (now consolidated in ss35 and 36 of Companies Act 1985) the position in these cases depended on the way in which the promoter signed the contract - a signature 'on behalf of' the company made the promoter personally liable, whereas a signature purely to authenticate the company's agreement did not. This highly unsatisfactory distinction no longer exists, for the promoter is now presumed to be liable on the contract unless there is an agreement to the contrary. *Phonogram* v *Lane* (1982) is authority for saying that the new wording entirely disposes of the former distinction. The consequence of this is that the company is never liable on a pre-incorporation contract. It may after incorporation make a new contract on the same terms but with itself as party in place of the promoter. It does not appear that this has been done here ('taking over the liabilities of Francis' looks like an attempt to ratify the pre-incorporation contract, and this cannot be done (*Melhado* v *Porto Alegre Railway Co* (1874)) and in consequence the company is not liable on this contract - Junk Bros will have to sue Francis personally.

With regard to Harry's expenses, there would normally be a provision in the articles allowing the directors to pay such expenses. This is not a contract - if the money were not paid Harry could not sue - but it is sufficient authority for the directors, and it is most unlikely that the liquidator would succeed in recovering these sums.

So far as the prospectus is concerned, the problem is that no disclosure has been made of the land deal, and James has not been mentioned as being a promoter. As regards the purchase of track the position depends upon whether James was already a promoter of the company when he bought it; if so, he cannot resell to the company at a profit (*Gluckstein* v *Barnes* (1900)), but if he was not a promoter at that point, then his only duty is to make proper disclosure of the transaction in the prospectus: *Omnium Electric Palaces Ltd* v *Baines* (1914). If the liquidator considers that James is in breach of his duties in connection with this transaction, then he may require James to hand over any profit which he has made.

The question of criminal liability for defective prospectuses is also of some importance here, though it must be noted that for the most part this will be of little use to the liquidator, since it will not allow him to increase the assets of the company. An officer of the company who allows the issue of a misleading prospectus may be guilty of an offence under s19 of Theft Act 1968 (a prospectus may be misleading under this section by reason of omissions as well as by reason of inclusions: *R* v *Kyslant* (1932)). Dishonest concealment of material facts may also give rise to liability under the Financial Services Act, and the omission from the prospectus may well amount to this offence.

The promoters may also incur civil liabilities in damages to investors in the company if they have invested on the faith of a misleading prospectus, but these remedies are also of little interest to the liquidator.

QUESTION 3

Arthur and Bill decided to form a company, Arbill Ltd, to carry on the business of manufacturing and distributing skiing equipment. Solicitors were instructed to proceed with the registration of the company, but before the company was registered, Arthur and Bill set about making preparations. Arthur arranged for a loan of £100,000 to be made to him to be transferred to the company when formed and Bill ordered 'for the benefit of the prospective Arbill Ltd', 50 tons of steel costing £40,000. Bill also agreed to purchase premises, as the company's factory, for £25,000, paying a deposit from his own resources of £2,500. All these transactions took place in January and February 1985, the company was registered, with Arthur and Bill as the sole shareholders and directors. At the first shareholders meeting, a resolution was passed by the company 'ratifying all pre-incorporation contracts' and at the second meeting, a resolution was passed ratifying the receipt by Arthur and Bill 'in their own names and for their own benefit, the company having no interest therein', of profits totalling £50,000 arising from the purchase and sale of land adjoining the company's factory.

In May, the company, having been very badly managed, went into insolvent liquidation.

Discuss the following:

a)   The bank wishes to recover its loan of £100,000.

b)   The steel has not yet been delivered, but the suppliers are anxious to do so since the price of steel has dropped substantially since it concluded the contract with Bill.

c)   The premises which were agreed to be purchased as the company's factory have risen steeply in value. The vendor wishes to avoid the obligation of completing the transaction by conveying the land. Bill, on the other hand, is anxious to take transfer of the land in his own name, while the liquidator is claiming the land for the company.

d)   The liquidator is anxious to recover the £50,000 taken by Arthur and Bill as profit from the purchase and sale of the adjoining property.

University of London LLB Examination
(for External Students) Company Law June 1985 Q5

General comment

This next question again calls for advice to the liquidator, but also deals with the position of other parties. It is an exceptionally complex problem on this area of the law, raising several related but separate issues. It is therefore especially important to be both clear and logical when approaching this question.

Skeleton solution

A is liable on the pre-incorporation contract (CA 1985 s36) - company can never be liable without a new contract.

B is liable - no clear agreement that he should be exempt from liability.

Promoter's duties - question whether B contracted on own behalf or as trustee for company - company probably entitled to benefit of contract.

Promoter's duty not to make secret profit - unclear whether disclosure has been made - possible ratification by General Meeting.

Suggested solution

This question concerns pre-incorporation contracts and the duties of promoters. Until the Certificate of Incorporation is issued the company has no legal existence, but it is usually necessary for contracts to be made on the company's behalf before that time as a preparation for the commencement of business. Problems arise concerning the enforcability of those contracts against the company. Turning to the specific issues in the question:

a)   The bank will wish to recover its loan from Arthur and/or the company. Arthur is a promoter within *Twycross* v *Grant* (1877), but it is not possible for him to assign the arrangement to the company after its formation because the company cannot adopt or ratify a pre-incorporation contract: *Natal Land Co* v *Pauline Colliery Syndicate* (1904); *Howard* v *Patent Ivory Manufacturing Co* (1888). The reason advanced for this is that the principal was not in existence at the time when the agent purported to contract on its behalf. Although this rationale is not very satisfactory, the rule of law is well established. Consequently the company is never liable on a pre-incorporation contract. The only way to bind the company is by a new contract on exactly the same terms (*Melhado* v *Porto Alegre Railway Co* (1874)), and this does not appear to have been done here.

Arthur's liability is established beyond doubt by Companies Act (CA) 1985 s36(4). The bank's best course is therefore to proceed against Arthur personally.

b)   Bill has ordered steel for the unformed company, and the suppliers wish to hold him to the contract. CA 1985 s36(4) is again relevant. This provides that a promoter who makes a pre-incorporation contract is personally liable on it subject to any agreement to the contrary. Such agreement must be clearly expressed (*Phonogram* v *Lane* (1982), per Lord Denning) and cannot be inferred merely from the way in which he promoter signs the contract. This last point reverses the old rule that the promoter's liability depended upon the form of words used in signing the contract. It is therefore concluded that in the present case Bill will be personally liable.

c)   This part of the question raises the issue of promoters' duties. As a matter of basic contract law, if contracts have been exchanged, then the vendor must complete, but otherwise there is no binding contract to be enforced. The problem is to decide who is entitled to the benefit of the contract, and this depends on the capacity in which the promoter held the benefit of the contract. If he was trustee for the unformed company, then the company is entitled to the benefit of the contract - *Omnium Electric Palaces Ltd* v *Baines* (1914) - but if he contracted on his own behalf, he is entitled to retain the benefit of the contract for himself. In the present case it is relevant that Bill provided the deposit out of his own resources, but this is not conclusive, not least since it is hard to see where else the money could have come from. The liquidator has at least an arguable case that the company is entitled to the benefit of this contract.

d)   Arthur and Bill have made a profit from the sale of property adjoining the factory. Promoters stand in a fiduciary position to the company, and this means that they must not make a secret profit. However, there is no breach of duty where full and frank disclosure is made in advance; even where this has not been done, the company in General Meeting may subsequently ratify the transaction, again provided that proper disclosure is made: *Gluckstein* v *Barnes* (1900); *Lagunas Nitrate Co* v *Lagunas Syndicate Ltd* (1899). In the present case it is not clear whether proper disclosure has been made. If it has not, then the liquidator may claim the profits, but otherwise Arthur and Bill will be entitled to retain the £50,000.

QUESTION 4

Gerald, Jill and Harry form a syndicate. They pool their redundancy money and buy catering equipment. They run a business from an old school kitchen which Jill bought for £500. They supply cakes and pies to local hotels. The business is successful and they decide to form a company. Jill sells the kitchen to the company for £2,000. Gerald buys 3 vans for £5,000 each and resells two of them to the company at that price. He discovers that the third van is more valuable than he suspected because it has £1,000 pounds worth of refrigerator equipment in it. Gerald decides to keep that van for his own company which runs a full catering service in the area.

Meanwhile Harry asks British Telecom to install a phone, telling them that the company, when formed, will take over the liabilities in respect of phone bills. Henry pays £100 deposit for the installation of the phone. The company is incorporated and Harry, Jill and Gerald are named as sole directors. Harry phones British Telecom and instructs them to bill the company in future. They do so but £500 worth of bills remain unpaid.

The company has now failed and a liquidator has been appointed. Advise all parties as to their rights and liabilities.

University of London LLB Examination
(for External Students) Company Law June 1987 Q5

General comment

In this case students are required to advise the liquidator and the promoters.

Skeleton solution

Definition of promoter - promoters' fiduciary duties - duties of disclosure - need to disclose to independent board. J's contract may be rescinded if no disclosure made - or profit may be recovered from promoter.

G is in breach of fiduciary duty - may be liable in damages.

H is liable on pre-incorporation contract, as no agreement to contrary - company cannot be liable without new contract.

Suggested solution

This question concerns pre-incorporation contracts and the duties of promoters. 'Promoters' here means someone who is engaged in taking the necessary steps to form a company and to set it in motion (*Twycross* v *Grant* (1877)). There are three situations with which the liquidator will need to be concerned - Jill's sale of the kitchen to the company, Gerald's sale of the vans and his retention of one of them and Harry's dealings with British Telecom.

Jill, as a promoter, owes fiduciary duties to the company. One consequence of this is that she is not allowed to make a secret profit from the company, and must account to the company for any secret profit made. However, the principle is not infringed if she makes full disclosure of the transaction to an independent Board and obtains its consen: *Erlanger* v *New Sombrero Phosphate Co* (1878). The difficulty with this principle is to decide what amounts to an independent Board of Directors. It is though that this expression must mean persons other than the promoters themselves, so that Harry, Jill and Gerald would not qualify as such. An alternative, suggested in *Salomon* v *Salomon* (1897), is full disclosure to the members of the company.

Unfortunately, the members and the directors are here the same people, but it may be that dislcosure to the members as such will suffice. It is unclear how much Harry and Gerald knew of Jill's dealings. If they had no knowledge, then the liquidator may seek to rescind the contract, provided of course that the company is in a position to make restitution in integrum by handing back what it has received under the contract. The right to rescind (which is an equitable right) may also be lost if the company has subsequently ratified the contract or has used the asset in the course of its business after learning of Jill's breach of duty: *Lagunas Nitrate Co* v *Lagunas Syndicate Ltd* (1899). As an alternative to rescission, the liquidator may recover the profit from the promoter, provided that it was acquired by her after she became a promoter (*Gluckstein* v *Barnes* (1900)); otherwise the company may be able to claim damages for breach of the promoter's duty of skill and care to the company. Such a breach may be committed where the promoter causes the company to buy an asset at an overvalue: *Re Leeds and Hanley Theatre of Varieties* (1902). A purchase of this kind from a member of the company may also be an unlawful distribution of the company's assets, and the distribution may be recovered from the shareholder under Companies Act (CA) 1985 s277.

Gerald has not made a profit on the sale of the vans to the company, but appears to be in breach of his fiduciary duties in that he has allowed a conflict of interest to develop because he is carrying on a business which is at least partially in competition with that of the company. It is thought that the position of a promoter here is similar to that of a director - both are fiduciaries - and *Bell* v *Lever Brothers* (1933) states that a director may run a competing company, but may not use confidential information or opportunity acquired in one capacity in order to benefit himself in another. If the liquidator can prove that Gerald acquired the vans in the course of his promotion of the company and then benefitted another company, he may be able to require Gerald to account for any profit made as a result of this breach of duty. Gerald also appears to be in breach of his duty of skill and care in not selling the refrigerated van to the company, since this may have damaged the efficient running of the company.

Harry has made a pre-incorporation contract. The position is now governed by CA 1985 s36(4), which makes the promoter personally liable on contracts of this kind unless there is agreement to the contrary (the company cannot be liable because it is considered unable to ratify a contract which was made on its behalf before it came into existence: *Kelner* v *Baxter* (1866)). The agreement to the contrary must surely be an agreement with the creditor rather than with the company which by definition does not exist at the time. There is no evidence of any such agreement here, and the result must be that Harry is liable to pay the £500. The only way in which the company could become liable would be by making a new contract on the same terms as that made by the promoter, and this has not happened here.

Type 2: Questions on prospectuses only

General comment

The last two questions from the London paper deal only with prospectuses. Question 5 is a straightforward problem on liability for defective prospectuses. Question 6 is more tricky in that it asks for a comparison between the rules under CA 1985 and the special rules for listed companies contained in the Financial Services Act 1986.

QUESTION 5

The three partners of Terco are Bill, Harold and Jane. The partnership specialises in setting up shops on garage forecourts. Bill, Harold and Jane decide to turn the business into a public company. At that time the partnership owned four garage forecourt shops situated along a very busy road. They were negotiating with PB plc, a petrol company, for setting up a shop on a fifth site along the same route. That site was situated at a very busy junction between two roads. Harold brought the land between the two roads when the plan to build the junction was first revealed. He paid only £5,000 as the farmer who owned the site expected it to be made useless by the proximity of the road junction.

In the prospectus issued at the floating of Terco plc it is stated that the company has acquired the site for 'less than the market price of land in that area'. The company has paid Harold £5,000 cash and issued £10,000 worth of shares to him. The market price in that area of prime farming land would be £20,000.

Bill is the other partner in charge of planning applications.

He is responsible for the statement in the prospectus that 'when planning permission is granted this will be a prime site for the proposed development'. The prospectus further states that Bill, Harold and Jane will become directors of Terco plc and describes them as specialists in the field. None have any formal qualifications. Bill and Jane become directors but Harold suffers a heart attack and declines to become a director on health grounds. Albert acquires 1,000 shares in the company. The company fails to get permission for the site, petrol strikes cause loss of business for the company and one year after flotation the shares are worth only 10p each. The company is on the verge of insolvent liquidation.

1) Advise Albert on any remedies he may have.

2) If a liquidator is appointed advise what action he should take.

University of London LLB Examination
(for External Students) Company Law June 1985 Q7

General comment

This is a question which requires candidates to advise both an investor and the liquidator.

Skeleton solution

A needs to know about civil remedies - deceit may not be provable - use Misrepresentation Act 1967 instead for action against company - directors possibly liable under *Hedley Byrne*. If A is a subscriber, sue promoters for deficiences in prospectus - liquidator should bring misfeasance action - also investigate H's sale of land to the company.

Suggested solution

Albert has acquired 1,000 shares in Terco Ltd. He is to be advised on liabilities in relation to a defective prospectus. There are possible criminal liabilities (s19 Theft Act 1968, as well as Companies Act 1985 and Financial Services Act (FSA) 1986) but Albert will be more interested in his possible civil remedies, principally damages and/or rescission of the contract for the shares. Remedies under Part III Chapter I of the Companies Act 1985 are also relevant.

It will be difficult to prove deceit, since this is available only where a misstatement of fact is made fraudulently, ie with knowledge that it is false or recklessly as to whether or not it is true. The burden of proof is a heavy one, and Albert would do better to use s2(1) Misrepresentation Act 1967 which allows an action for damages if a person enters into a contract after a misrepresentation has been made by the other party thereto. In this case the statements regarding the value of the land and the description of the directors may well amount to misstatements. A duty under *Hedley Byrne* v *Heller* (1963) may also arise in connection with the statement regarding the planning application, since Bill is in charge of such matters, though it is worth observing that at the present day the trend of the law seems to be away from recognising such duties.

So far as the 1967 Act is concerned, the company could be liable, but it does not appear that directors or experts could, since they are not parties to the eventual contract for the sale of the shares. By contrast, *Hedley Byrne* liability could in theory fall on a director or an expert, since Albert relies on them and not on the company.

A good deal depends upon whether Albert is an original subscriber for the shares or whether he is a subsequent purchaser. In the former event the prospectus is addressed to him and he can sue for its defects (*Peek* v *Gurney* (1873)) but in the latter event he cannot sue unless the prospectus was intended to induce market dealings: *Andrews* v *Mockford* (1896).

Under s166 FSA 1986 once Albert (assuming that he is a subscriber) proves that he has sustained damage by reason of untrue statements in the prospectus his action will succeed unless the defendant disproves responsibility for the prospectus, or proves that he honestly and reasonably believed up until the time of allotment that the statement was true. The company cannot be made liable under this provision - rather, liability falls on every person who authorised himself to be named and who is named as a director, upon promoters and upon every person who authorised the issue of the prospectus. Bill, Harold and Jane clearly fall within this category; they appear to have no defence available since they have not dissociated themselves from the prospectus nor have they proved the necessary belief in its accuracy.

Damages may also be claimed from directors and promoters (but not the company) for the omission from the prospectus of information required to be included under FSA s162.

In summary, Albert's remedies are rescission against the company and/or damages against Bill, Harold and Jane. The liquidator should bring an action under Insolvency Act s212 against the directors for misfeasance, since the company's present position appears to be due to the directors' mishandling of its affairs. It would also be worth investigating the sale of land by Harold to the company, since this may be voidable on the grounds of being a breach of the promoter's fiduciary duty not to make a secret profit from promoting the company: *Gluckstein* v *Barnes* (1900).

QUESTION 6

Fred, Ken and George are the directors of Brightlite Ltd. That company has for some years been involved in the manufacture of a new light bulb which contains zero gas. This produces a brighter, longer lasting bulb. The compnay has been successful and the directors decide to expand by becoming a public company, issuing one hundred thousand £1 shares, and obtaining a listing on the Stock Exchange.

The directors issue a prospectus which explains the benefits of the use of zero gas. It names Fred, Ken and George as directors but makes no mention of the assistance given in the promotion of the company by Cecil, who last year was the subject of a disqualification order made by the court. The order was made for a period of three years. Three days before the shares are to be issued, Fred receives a report from Jill, an expert attached to the company, which contained details of early experiments which could show a slight carcinogenic effect caused by long exposure to zero gas. Fred believes the report to be of little significance and mentions it to no-one. Bill buys £5,000 of shares from the company. Harry buys £5,000 of shares three months later on the Stock Exchange.

Zero gas has now been banned by the government because of its alleged carcinogenic effect and the shares in the company are worthless.

Explain what courses of action would be open to Bill and Harry under the Companies Act 1985 and compare them to the courses of action available under the Financial Services Act 1986.

University of London LLB Examination
(for External Students) Company Law June 1988 Q6

Skeleton solution

Directors and promoters responsible for accuracy of prospectus - also experts - B is original subscriber, so can sue under CA 1985 s67 - note possible deficiencies of prospectus, but also difficulties of proof and construction - distinguish between the different positions of the various defendants - note also FSA 1986 which extends the possible liabilities.

Suggested solution

Under Companies Act (CA) 1985 s67 the primary responsibility for the accuracy of a company's prospectus rests with the directors. They will be liable to pay compensation to all persons who subscribe for shares (ie buy them from the company on allotment) for any loss or damage resulting from a misleading statement. The claim may be brought against any director or promoter or anyone who was a party to the issue of the prospectus (or the part of it which contained the misleading statement) and against any person who authorised the issue of the prospectus. This would certainly include Fred, Ken and George. In addition, Jill may be liable as an expert if she consents to the issue of a misleading prospectus. Cecil will be potentially liable under s15 Company Directors Disqualification Act 1986 if he is personally involved as a promoter - this is a question of fact. He may also be fined and/or imprisoned for acting in contravention of the disqualification order.

The claim under CA 1985 must be brought by someone who has subscribed for shares directly from the company ie Bill. He may sue in respect of a false statement upon which he has relied. There seem here to be two material omissions - the failure to disclose Cecil's disqualification order and failure to mention the possible carcinogenic effect of the gas. It might be possible to construe from the latter a positive statement that the gas is safe, but this is by no means clear cut. Under CA 1985 s71 a statement is false if it is misleading in the form and context in which it appears.

Various defences are available. The defendant may escape liability if he honestly and reasonably believed the statement to be true. Here, only Fred knows of Jill's report so Ken and George may be able to rely on this defence if they can show that they made reasonable enquiries about the truth of the statement. It seems highly improbable that Fred can rely on this defence. Fred should have withdrawn his consent to act as a director or should have made a disclaimer about the report. This would have given him a defence. The other directors, on finding out the truth from Jill's report, should have withdrawn their consent to the prospectus.

The position under CA 1985 therefore seems to be that Bill (but only Bill) may sue Fred for compensation. The damages will be the same as in an action for deceit. Ken, George and Jill may perhaps be liable for failing to withdraw their consent to the prospectus, or in Jill's case to any report of hers contained in the prospectus.

In relation to companies with a Stock Exchange listing the position is now governed by the Financial Services Act 1986. Under that Act the following categories of persons may be responsible for the contents of a prospectus:

a)   the issuer of the securities;

b)   the directors of the issuing company at the time when the particulars are submitted to the listing committee;

c)   persons named in the listing particulars as having authorised this;

d)   anybody else who has assumed responsiblity for all or any part of the particulars.

Section 150 of the Act provides a remedy to an investor who acquires securities or an interest in them and suffers loss by reason of false or misleading information in the listing particulars. This provision differs materially from that under CA 1985 in that it expressly imposes liability for omissions as well as for inclusions. In addition the remedy extends to subsequent purchasers of the shares on the open market, whereas under CA 1985 it is limited to the original subscribers for the shares.

FSA s151 provides various defences. It is a defence to show an honest and reasonable belief that a statement was true or that an omission was properly made. Similarly it is a defence if a correction was published as soon as possible or if the person who suffered the loss acquired the securities with knowledge of the omission.

The position under FSA therefore appears to be that both Bill and Harry will succeed against Fred, Ken and George. Cecil may also be liable as a promoter, and Jill may be liable in respect of any expert statement in the listing particulars.

Type 3: Essay questions

General comment

There is always the possibility of an essay question in this area. Three examples (written by the Editor August-October 1989) are given below, one on prospectuses, one on the general duties of promoters, one on pre-incorporation contracts. It is more likely that an essay question would be restricted to one of these topics than that it would cover two or more of them, but the three essays below can readily be combined if necessary.

QUESTION 7

'The law now gives adequate protection to those who buy company shares on the faith of a prospectus'. Discuss.

Written by Editor
August 1989

Skeleton solution

General trend in favour of protecting purchasers. CA 1985 makes directors or promoters liable to anyone who suffers loss.

Financial Services Act applies to listed companies. Imposes liability on directors and others who vouch for accuracy of particulars, subject to limited defences.

Suggested solution

The law in this area has been subject to amendment in recent years. There is now a complex mixture of common law and statutory rules governing liability for misstatements in prospectuses.

Under Companies Act (CA) 1985 s67 the directors are responsible for the accuracy of a company's prospectus. They will be liable to pay compensation to all persons who subscribe for shares (ie buy them from the company on allotment) for any loss or damage resulting from a misleading statement. The claim may be brought against any director or promoter or anyone who was a party to the issue of the prospectus (or the part of it which contained the misleading statement) and against any person who authorised the issue of the prospectus.

Under CA 1985 s71 a statement is false if it is misleading in the form and context in which it appears.

The statute provides various defences; in particular the defendant may escape liability if he honestly and reasonably believed the statement to be true.

In relation to listed companies the position is now governed by the Financial Services Act 1986. Under that Act the following categories of persons may be responsible for the contents of a prospectus:

a)   the issuer of the securities;

b)   the directors of the issuing company at the time when the particulars are submitted to the listing committee;

c)   persons named in the listing particular as having authorised this;

d)   anybody else who has assumed responsiblity for all or any part of the particulars.

Section 150 of the Act provides a remedy to an investor who acquires securities or an interest in them and suffers loss by reason of false or misleading information in the listing particulars. This provision differs materially from that under CA 1985 in that it expressly imposes liability for omissions as well as for inclusions. In addition the remedy extends to subsequent purchasers of the shares on the open market, whereas under CA 1985 it is limited to the original subscribers for the shares.

FSA s151 provides various defences. It is a defence to show an honest and reasonable belief that a statement was true or that an omission was properly made. Similarly it is a defence if a correction was published as soon as possible or if the person who suffered the loss acquired the securities with knowledge of the omission.

QUESTION 8

What are the duties of a promoter in relation to his company, and what are the consequences of a breach of that duty?

Written by Editor
October 1989

Skeleton solution

Definitions of promoter - promoter's fiduciary duties - may be liable to company if full disclosure not made - transactions voidable or company may claim account of profits - promoter may not use information to his own advantage.

Suggested solution

A promoter has been judicially defined as someone who undertakes to form a company and to set it in motion: *Twycross* v *Grant* (1877) per Cockburn CJ. A promoter occupies a fiduciary position in relation to his company. This means that he must not act contrary to the interests of the company and must not make a secret profit from his position as promoter. In *Gluckstein* v *Barnes* (1900) the promoters sold assets to the company at a considerable profit to themselves without making any disclosure of the circumstances beyond a very brief and obscure mention in the prospectus. It was held that this was not adequate and that they were therefore liable to account to the company for the profit which they had made. The position would have been different if they had made full and frank disclosure and had had the transaction approved by the members. From the company's point of view an alternative to obtaining an account of any profit is to set aside the transaction under which the promoter sold assets to the company. Such a remedy is naturally subject to the usual rules governing rescission - the right may be lost by lapse of time or by affirmation, and will certainly be lost if the company is no longer able to make restitutio in integrum of the assets which it acquired.

The duty not to compete means that the promoter, like a director, must not use information or any opportunity which he acquires in his position as a promoter to make a profit for himself - rather he must turn it to the company's advantage. Again he can be required to account for any profit arising from a breach of this obligation. It is, however, sometimes difficult to tell whether a person has been acting as a promoter at the time of a particular transaction, and this is important since the fiduciary duties already described apply only to promoters acting as such.

QUESTION 9

'Section 36 of the Companies Act 1985 has put the law relating to pre-incorporation contracts on a satisfactory footing.' Do you agree?

Written by Editor
October 1989

Skeleton solution

Pre-1985 position: depended on form of words used in signing contract - s36(4) abolishes this distinction - promoter now personally liable in absence of contrary agreement - company never liable on original contract, but may be liable if new contract made - would be preferable to allow company to ratify original contract - contracting out of promoter's liability is also very difficult.

Suggested solution

Before the enactment of s36(4) (which was originally part of s9 of the European Communities Act 1972) the question whether the company was liable on a contract purportedly made on its behalf before its formation depended on the way in which the contract was signed. If it was signed 'for and on behalf of the company' then this was treated as purported agency, and was not valid because there can be no agency whilst the principal is not in existence: *Kelner* v *Baxter* (1866). By contrast, where the promoter signed merely to 'authenticate' the company's participation, the company was bound: *Melhado* v *Porto Alegre Railway Co* (1874). This was obviously an untenable distinction, and its removal by s36(4) is to be welcomed. However, it is also necessary to understand the changes which that provision has made. A pre-incorporation contract is now deemed to be made by the promoter as principal and he is therefore liable upon it as such (subject to any agreement to the contrary). The difficulty is that the company quite clearly is never liable, since it is not a party to the contract, and *Kelner* v *Baxter* prevents it from subsequently ratifying the contract once it has been incorporated. Consequently, the only way in which the company can take over the liability is by making an entirely new contract with the third party on the same terms as that made by the promoter. Regrettably, this has given rise to another untenable distinction; where the company seeks to ratify the original contract, such purported ratification is void, but where a new contract is made, this is effective. It is submitted that there is no good reason why the company should not be allowed to ratify pre-incorporation contracts if it so wishes, and that a further statutory amendment to this effect is desirable.

The question of agreements excluding the promoter's liability has also given rise to difficulty. In *Phonogram* v *Lane* (1982) it was said that the agreement must be express, and cannot be inferred from surrounding circumstances. It is very difficult to imagine in what circumstances a third party in an arm's length transaction would agree to a non-liability clause, given that such agreement does not serve to make the company liable. Consequently it seems that cases of contrary agreement will be extremely rare. Of course, this point would be of much less importance if companies could simply ratify pre-incorporation contracts.

6   CAPITAL

6.1 Introduction

6.2 Key points

6.3 Recent cases and statutes

6.4 Analysis of questions

6.5 Questions

6.1   Introduction

This chapter deals with the various rules governing the maintenance of a company's capital. These may be divided into three major sections, namely the prohibition on paying dividends except out of profits available for the purpose, the prohibition on re-purchasing a company's own shares and the prohibition (qualified under the modern law) on providing assistance for the purchase of the company's own shares.

6.2   Key points

a) *Dividends*

A company must not pay dividends except out of profits available for the purpose (CA 1985 s263). Profits available for the purpose are accumulated realised profits less accumulated realised losses.

Whether profits are to be treated as accumulated is decided according to the principles of good accounting practice (CA 1985 Sch 4 paras 88-91).

Part VIII of CA 1985 contains detailed rules relating to the treatment of revaluations of assets, and to the use of interim and initial accounts as the basis for a dividend.

Where an unlawful dividend is paid, a shareholder who knows of the unlawfulness may be required to repay the dividend to the company (CA 1985 s277).

Public companies are subject to a further restriction in that they may not pay a dividend if the result of doing so would be to reduce their net worth below the value of their issued capital (CA 1985 s264).

b) *Purchase of own shares*

The rules in this area were significantly relaxed by CA 1981, which varied the earlier very strict prohibitions on a company repurchasing its own shares.

By s159 a company may issue redeemable shares, ie shares which are expressed on the face of them to be redeemable, and these will then be redeemable in accordance with the terms and conditions attached to them at the time of issue.

However, a company must always have some shares which are not expressed to be redeemable.

Even where shares are not expressed to be redeemable, it may be possible to redeem them in accordance with s162, provided this procedure is authorised by the company's articles of association. The exact procedure to be followed need not be specified in the articles.

The shares of public companies may only be redeemed out of distributable profits or out of the proceeds of a fresh issue of shares made for the purpose of financing the purchase. Private companies have the further option of redeeming shares out of capital.

c)   *Assistance for purchase of own shares*

CA 1985 ss151-154 impose a general prohibition on a company providing financial assistance, whether directly or indirectly, for the purchase of its own shares.

At the same time s153 provides exemptions from the prohibition where the assistance is given as an incidental part of some larger purpose of the company and is given in good faith in the best interests of the company.

Section 151 additionally provides exemptions from the general prohibition which apply only to private companies. This section contains the relaxation of the rules introduced by the 1985 Act. Essentially private companies are exempt from the prohibition so long as they follow certain procedures (specified in ss155-158). These involve a statutory declaration by the directors that the company is solvent and will remain so after the giving of the assistance. The auditors must also produce a report supporting this contention. If the net assets of the company are to be reduced by the giving of the assistance, then the funds used must be distributable profits of the company (s155(2)).

Finally, the proposal must be approved by a Special Resolution of the General Meeting, except where the company proposing to give the assistance is a wholly-owned subsidiary of the company which is to receive the assistance.

6.3   Recent cases and statutes

The Companies Act 1985 significantly relaxed the rules governing purchase by a company of its own shares.

Precision Dippings Ltd v *Precision Dippings Marketing Ltd and Others* [1985] 3 WLR 812.

Aveling Barford Ltd v *Perion Ltd* (1989) Financial Times 29 April.

6.4   Analysis of questions

The subject of company capital has been a popular one on the London LLB External - it has appeared five times since 1983, four of the questions having been in essay form. It is, however, a topic of which students should be wary. Firstly, it can be presented in a number of forms. One of these concerns the rules against paying dividends except out of profits available for the purpose; another form of the question addresses itself to reductions of capital and the need to obtain the sanction of the court. The third area which may be set concerns payment for shares. Care is needed in distinguishing quite what the question is asking for, as in the first group of questions contained in this chapter. More commonly, the three areas may appear together, as in the second group of questions in this chapter. The second problem for students is that this is a technical area of the law, with a number of detailed rules. It is difficult to write adequtely about profit distribution without some knowledge of the accounting concepts of profit and realisations; this is a knowledge possessed by very few law students. It is also an area where a student who is ill-prepared has little hope of bluffing his way through. Proper knowledge of the technical rules is indispensable, and students who do not have it are advised to avoid this topic in the examination.

With those caveats in mind it is possible to go on and look at the questions which come up in this area.

6.5   Questions

Type 1: Questions on part of the topic

QUESTION 1

'Since the enactment of provisions legalising the purchase of its own shares it will no longer be necessary for a company to resort to the cumbersome statutory procedure of reducing its capital.' Discuss.

University of London LLB Examination
(for External Students) Company Law June 1983 Q3

General comment

The emphasis here is on reduction of capital, but the examiner has slanted the question by asking about the relationship between this and the purchase of a company's own shares.

Skeleton solution

General principle against purchase of own shares - some relaxation in CA 1981 - legitimate reasons for wanting to buy back shares - rules as to purchase - need to fund out of profits/proceeds of fresh issue - private company may fund purchase out of capital - approval of GM is also required - purchase is generally preferable to capital reduction, but may not always be possible if there are no profits.

Suggested solution

The old rule (established in *Trevor* v *Whitworth* (1887)) was that a company could not buy its own shares because to do so would amount to an unauthorised reduction of capital. This was confirmed, subject to specified limited exemptions by s35 of the 1980 Act. However, in the 1981 Act the law was changed (the current rules are collected in ss151 et seq of the 1985 Act) and the present regime is somewhat more liberal. There are a number of advantages to allowing a company to buy its own shares, and not all of these can be achieved by means of a reduction of capital. A company may be able to buy out a dissident shareholder or to retain family control or to buy out the estate of a deceased shareholder in a private company. Similarly, a shareholder-director who is retiring may be able to dispose of his holding in this way if there is no ready outside buyer in prospect. The same method may be adopted with the shares of employees who have received shares under a share incentive scheme (though at the present day the legal title to such shares is more commonly held by trustees). In recognition of these arguments the present law allows a company to re-purchase any of its own shares (including any redeemable shares) if authorised to do so by its own articles. In the case of shares which were issued as redeemable shares it is not necessary that the term and manner of purchase be determined by the articles.

In summary, the present rules prohibit purchases if only redeemable shares are left and prohibit the purchase of partly paid shares. The finance for the purchase must come from distributable profits or from the proceeds of a fresh issue of shares. Any premium paid for the shares should come out of profits or out of the share premium account. Where the purchase is funded out of profits an amount equal to the nominal value of the shares purchased must be transferred to the Capital Redemption Reserve (s170). A private company may purchase its shares out of capital by using the permissible capital payment (s171).

A resolution of the company in General Meeting is also required in order to authorise purchase of the company's shares. If the purchase is made off-market (which will necessarily be the case with a private company, but is relatively unlikely to happen in the case of a public company) or by means of a contingent purchase contract, then a special resolution is required; an ordinary resolution will suffice in the case of a market purchase.

The relative simplicity of the above procedure compared with that for a capital reduction (in particular the absence of any requirement to seek the court's approval) means that, given the choice, most companies are likely to favour purchasing rather than reducing capital. However, the choice will not always be available. Where the company has suffered significant losses it is appropriate to reduce the amount of capital since the original amount would no longer represent the amount to which creditors could look for payment. Alternatively, a company which has excessive assets should be allowed, subject to necessary protections for creditors, to reduce its share capital. Reductions of this kind, which affect all shareholders in proportion to their holdings, are more appropriately achieved by the capital reduction mechanism than by a re-purchase. A further point is that where the company has losses, there will be no profits to fund a purchase and it is unlikely that anyone will wish to take up new shares, so that reduction of capital will be the only viable mechanism. In cases of this kind it is appropriate to insist on capital reduction for the additional reason that the requirement to seek the sanction of the court allows the interests of creditors to be protected. It appears from *ex parte Westburn Sugar Refineries* (1951) that objections by creditors to the proposed reduction will carry more weight than objections by shareholders, though the class rights of shareholders must also be respected: *Re Old Silkstone Collieries* (1954), *Re Holders Investment Trust* (1971).

Thus it can be seen that the new re-purchase rules, although offering a simple and attractive mechanism, cannot entirely remove the need for using the reduction of capital procedure in certain cases.

QUESTION 2

'Companies are forbidden to make any distribution of dividends except out of profits legally available for this purpose.' Discuss the development and interpretation of this principle, both by the courts and the legislature.

University of London LLB Examination
(for External Students) Company Law June 1985 Q2

General comment

At first sight this looks to be a clear (if difficult) question about the modern rules on distributions contained in Part VIII of the 1985 Act. Closer reading of the question shows, however, that a further twist has been inserted. The judicial development of this doctrine occurred before the present statutory provisions were introduced in 1980. Consequently the candidate is required to discuss both the pre-1980 case law and the current legislative provisions, probably in roughly equal proportions.

Skeleton solution

Old rule was: no dividend out of capital. New rule is: no dividend except out of available profit. New rule is more restrictive, since accounting periods are not treated in isolation. Available profits are accumulated realised profits less accumulated realised losses. Realisation is determined according to accounting principles. Profit and loss not defined by statute. Public companies subject to additional restrictions.

Suggested solution

The principle stated in the question is clearly based very closely on the wording of s263 of the 1985 Act, and is a good statement of the general principle (there are exceptions) which applies under the present law. Before 1980, when the present rules were introduced, the rule was more accurately stated as being that dividends could not be paid out of capital since this would offend the capital maintenance doctrine: *Flitcroft's Case* (1882); *Verner v Commercial and General Investment Trust* (1894). This was a much narrower doctrine than that which now prevails. In particular where there was a profit on revenue account in the current year, a dividend could be paid even though losses on previous years had not been made up: *Ammonia Soda Co Ltd v Chamberlain* (1918). In addition, a surplus arising on a revaluation of fixed assets which were not to be sold could be distributed, since this surplus would be additional to the company's issued capital, so that the capital maintenance doctrine was not infringed - *Dimbula Valley (Ceylon) Tea Co v Laurie* (1961). The court was not concerned with issues as to the prudence of a distribution: *Lee v Neuchatel Asphalte Co* (1889). Essentially the court treated each accounting period in isolation. However, increasing difficulty was felt with these rules, partly because they were significantly at variance with good accounting practice and partly because of pressure from the EEC for the harmonisation of company law. New rules were consequently introduced in 1980, and these are now consolidated in Part VIII of the 1985 Act.

The general principle under the new provisions is that stated in the question. It is important to be aware that 'distribution' here does not cover all forms of distribution of a company's assets. Section 263 of the 1985 Act excludes from the definition the issue of bonus shares, purchase of own shares, payments in a reduction of capital and distributions of assets in a winding-up. All these are covered by separate specific provisions of the 1985 Act. All other forms of distribution are included, however, and it may be observed that distributions by way of sales at an undervalue to a member are covered, as well as declarations of dividends.

The next question to ask is what are 'profits available for the purpose'? Section 263 defines these as accumulated realised profits less accumulated realised losses. This reverses the *Dimbula Valley* rule, since one accounting period must be taken with another. Only the net profits are available for distribution, since sums previously distributed must be taken into account in making the calculation. The use of the term 'realised' in the new rule is also significant. A profit achieved by revaluing a fixed asset is not a realised profit, and therefore cannot be taken into account (subject to certain specified exceptions). Realisation is to be determined according to the notions of good accounting practice (Sch 4 Para 88) which is one further step along the path of allowing accounting notions to prevail for legal purposes.

The remaining element in the definition is that of 'profit' and 'loss'. These terms are not defined, and it appears that the earlier, rather unsatisfactory authorities, such as *Re Oxford Benefit Building and Investment Society* (1886) (which turns on the particular articles of the Society) and *Re Spanish Prospecting Co Ltd* (1911) remain good law in this context. This point may be of little importance, however; even if it can be determined that there is a profit or loss according to these rules, it will still be necesary to decide whether there has been realisation, and this, as explained above, is determined according to accountancy principles.

Public companies are subject to the additional restrictions imposed by s264. They may make distributions only to the extent that their net assets after the distribution are not less than the amount of their called-up share capital plus their undistributable reserves: the last phrase includes the share premium account and the capital redemption reserve.

The accounts used to justify a distribution are the 'relevant accounts'. These will usually be the last annual accounts, but interim accounts may sometimes be used.

Under s277 the recipient of an unlawful distribution who is a shareholder is liable to repay it to the company if he had reason to know that the distribution was unlawful. *Re Aveling Barford Ltd* (1989) confirms that the position is the same where the recipient is not a shareholder.

Further restrictions on distributions may be imposed by the memorandum or the articles, but neither may provide any exemption from the requirements of Part VIII of the Act.

It can thus be seen that the new law differs radically from the old. In particular, it is much more interventionist and restrictive. There is as yet very little authority on the new rules, and it should be clear from the above that authorities on the pre-1980 rules must now be treated with great caution.

QUESTION 3

Outline the rules governing payment for a company's shares. How well do these rules serve to ensure that the company's capital is maintained?

Written by Editor
October 1989

General comment

This question illustrates the way in which the rules on payment for shares could be examined. It is deliberately divided into two parts. The first calls for a straightforward account of the prohibition on issuing shares at a discount and the Table A rules on making further calls. The second part is more analytical, calling on students to evaluate these rules from the point of view of the doctrine of capital maintenance. A moderate pass can be obtained by concentrating on the first part, but a good answer will need to deal satisfactorily with the second part as well. A further complication is that the rules as to payment for shares cover both the prohibition on financial assistance and the rules relating to the method of payment by the allottee in ss103-108 of the 1985 Act.

Skeleton solution

Two areas: financial assistance and methods of payment.

Financial assistance generally forbidden, but there are some statutory exceptions, though the drafting of these is not satisfactory.

Issue at discount generally forbidden. Minimum 25% payable on allotment. May not issue in return for promise to perform services. These rules are generally clear and well-conceived.

Suggested solution

This question is concerned with the rules which prevent a company from giving financial assistance for the purchase of its own shares and with the rules governing the way in which the allottee provides consideration for the shares allotted to him. These rules, which form part of the rules relating to the maintenance of a company's capital, are intended to protect creditors - who naturally look to a company's capital as a fund from which they can be paid - from the risk that the fund will be less than it appears because the company has recycled its existing capital to fund the issue of new capital.

The restrictions on the provision of financial assistance must also be understood in the context of the restrictions on a company buying its own shares; in the days when such purchases were strictly forbidden it would obviously have been absurd to allow the provision of assistance since that would have been a simple and obvious way of evading the spirit of the prohibition on purchase. With the relaxation of the rules on purchase of own shares it has become necessary to relax the rules on providing assistance, though the two sets of rules are not now in harmony.

The general prohibition on financial assistance is found in s151 of the 1985 Act, but there are exceptions. Under ss155-157 financial assistance may be given where the directors make a statutory declaration as to the company's present and future solvency and the transaction is approved by a Special Resolution of the company in general meeting.

More confusing, and less satisfactory, are the exceptions in ss152-154. If assistance is given bona fide and not for the purpose of enabling a person to buy shares in the company, then the prohibition does not apply; nor does it apply if the assistance was given as an incidental part of some larger transaction and bona fide in the best interests of the company. These exemptions are vague and couched in subjective language. They are also liable to permit the giving of assistance in situations where this is capable of operating prejudicially upon creditors. A major difficulty in this area is that there are criminal sanctions for the giving of prohibited assistance, and the drafting of these exemptions reflects that - the intention of potential defendants has been taken into account rather than the effect of what they do. It is submitted that a better approach would have been to provide that in these situations no offence is committed, but those receiving the assistance remain liable to repay it to the company.

Turning to the rules on payment by the allottee, it can be seen that the intention is to ensure that the company receives proper value for its shares. Thus, the issue of shares at a discount is entirely forbidden. In the case of public companies there are further restrictions. Such a company may not accept as payment an undertaking to perform services, nor any undertaking which may be performed more than five years after allotment. At least 25% of the nominal value of the share (plus the whole of any premium) must be paid on allotment and non-cash consideration can be accepted only after an expert's report as to the value of that consideration has been obtained and served on the company and the proposed allottee. There is criminal liability for breach of these requirements.

In summary it must be said that the rules as to financial assistance are not very satisfactory. They do not relate well to the rules on purchase of own shares, and there are undesirable loopholes through which harmful transactions may be protected. If the maintenance of the company's capital is to be taken seriously, then further statutory reform is required. By contrast, the rules on payment by the allottee appear to be clear and sensible. There does not seem to be any particular difficulty remaining in this area.

Type 2: Questions on the whole of the topic

QUESTION 4(a)

'The rules governing use by a company of its capital are strict and effective.' Discuss.

University of London LLB Examination
(for External Students) Company Law June 1986 Q2

QUESTION 4(b)

'The legislature and the courts go to great lengths to compel a company to maintain its capital.' Discuss.

University of London LLB Examination
(for External Students) Company Law June 1987 Q2

General comment

These two questions may conveniently be considered together. Although they are differently worded, both are clearly asking for a general consideration of the rules relating to the maintenance of capital.

Skeleton solution

Capital maintenance doctrine aims to protect creditors. Four limits: prohibition on purchasing own shares; prohibition on giving financial assistance; restrictions on distributions; rules as to payment for shares. First two have become more lenient in recent years, whereas third has become stricter. Generally, the problem of capital maintenance is well-recognised, but the legislation is somewhat piecemeal.

Suggested solution

The core of a company is its capital, by which is meant the fund contributed by shareholders (or by creditors in the case of loan capital) which is required as a guarantee fund. In theory the creditors are able to look to this fund for the payment of their debts if the company runs into financial difficulty. This concept would obviously be undermined if the company were allowed to return that capital to the people who have provided it, and the doctrine of capital maintenance therefore lays down a general rule that returns of capital to the members are prohibited, though, as is explained below, there are certain exceptions to this rule.

There are four limbs to the doctrine of capital maintenance. The first is that a company may not buy its own shares (*Trevor* v *Whitworth* (1887)) the second is that a company may not provide financial assistance to another for the purchase of its own shares (Companies Act (CA) 1985 ss151-157), the third is that distributions of a company's assets may only be made out of profits available for the purpose (CA 1985 Part VIII) and the fourth concerns the way in which consideration for shares is provided.

Turning to the first of these rules, it should be observed that the 1981 Act (now consolidated in the 1985 Act) relaxed the prohibition somewhat. Before that time purchase of a company's own shares was almost entirely prohibited, but in 1981 companies were given the power to issue redeemable shares as well as a general power to purchase their own shares subject to safeguards aimed at protecting creditors. There are a number of situations where it is useful to allow companies to re-purchase their own shares (dealing with retiring or dissentient shareholders may be cited as examples). Such purchases must normally be financed out of distributable profits or out of the proceeds of a fresh issue of shares. In addition the nominal value of the shares purchased must be paid into an account within the company's books entitled the 'capital redemption reserve'. A further safeguard is that the purchase must be approved by the company in general meeting; in the case of a private company the amount which may be expended in such purchases is also strictly defined (CA 1985 s171).

Financial assistance for the purchase of shares is generally prohibited under s151, but here again the rules are more lenient than they used to be. Such assistance is permitted if approved by a Special Resolution of the company after the directors have made a Statutory Declaration as to the company's solvency. More contentiously, there are exceptions where the assistance was given in good faith and not for the purpose of assisting in such a purchase (as where the recipient misuses money entrusted to him) or where it was given in good faith but as an incidental part of some larger purpose. These exemptions, which are apparently necessitated by the imposition of criminal sanctions for the wrongful giving of such assistance, provide loopholes which do much to weaken the effect of the general prohibiton.

The rules as to the making of distributions (which means primarily but not exclusively dividends) date from 1980; exceptionally in the present context the new rules are stricter than the old, which merely forbade the paying of dividends out of capital. Profits available for the purpose are accumulated realised profits less accumulated realised losses, so that one accounting period must be taken with another; realisation is determined according to good accountancy practice. The new rules go a long way to ensuring that the capital of the company is not dissipated by improper dividend payments. If payments are made in breach of these rules, a member who received a payment with actual or constructive knowledge of its unlawfulness is liable to repay it to the company (s277). The same result is reached if the distribution is made to a non-member: *Re Aveling Barford Ltd* (1989).

The rules as to payment for shares also date from 1980. They relate to the way in which a company, particularly a public company, should be paid for its shares. For instance, a public company cannot accept an undertaking to perform services, nor an undertaking which may be performed more than five years after allotment: both these methods are obviously open to abuse. A public company must receive at least 25% of the nominal value of the share (as well as the whole of any premium) on allotment; before it can accept any non-cash consideration an expert's report on the value of that consideration must be obtained and copies must be served on the company and the proposed allottee. The issuing of shares at a discount is now prohibited for all companies. There is criminal liability for the breach of these provisions.

In summary it may be said that the importance of capital maintenance is well recognised, though there are certain exceptions introduced in recent years and subject to the safeguards necessary to protect creditors. Reductions of capital may also be sanctioned by the court, but again permission will not be given unless creditors' interests are adequately protected.

QUESTION 5

In 1979 Excelsior plc made a net trading loss of £1,500,000 and in 1980 another loss of £1,000,000. In 1981, however, it made a profit of £1,000,000 and entered into negotiations to purchase a factory from Henry. The price was eventually agreed at £500,000 despite the fact that valuers appointed by Excelsior assessed the factory's value at £400,000. The directors of Excelsior decided to pay the price asked by Henry because they considered that the factory would considerably increase the company's profitability over the next few years. The purchase price was paid partly in cash (£200,000) and partly by the issue to Henry of 300,000 £1 shares, which issue was made concurrently with a rights issue made by the company to its existing shareholders of 1 share at par for each share held. James, one of the directors of Excelsior, who held 100,000 shares wanted to take up the rights issue, but was unable to raise the cash. He therefore negotiated with the company to defer payment in respect of his acceptance of the rights issue pending the declaration by the company of a dividend. At the end of 1982 the company in fact declared a dividend in respect of the entire profit made in 1981 and this enabled James to pay the company the amount owing in respect of the rights issue. In 1983, the company was compulsorily wound up.

Advise the liquidator.

University of London LLB Examination
(for External Students) Company Law June 1984 Q8

General comment

This question is somewthing of a rarity - a problem question on the maintenance of capital.

Skeleton solution

Purchase of factory - valuation rules - consequences of breach - duty to pay in cash.

Dividends - losses of previous years must be made good before dividend can be paid - this has not been done - liquidator can require repayment from any shareholder who was aware of this.

Financial assistance - disguised return of capital prohibited - there has probably been a breach here - liquidator should be advised to sue James.

Suggested solution

Three issues arise in this problem: the provision of financial assistance for the purchase of a company's shares, the declaration of dividends and payment for shares.

The factory has been purchased from Henry in cash and through the issue of 300,000 £1 shares. Under s103 Companies Act 1985 a company is forbidden to allot shares as fully or partly paid-up for non-cash consideration unless the consideration has been valued by an independent expert within the past six months and a copy of the report has been served on the company and the proposed allottee. If this requirement is contravened the allottee is liable to the company for an amount equal to the nominal value of the shares plus any premium thereon (a subsequent holder of the shares will be similarly liable unless he is a bona fide purchaser for value without notice of the contravention of s103). The fact that the directors paid an extra £100,000 for the factory in the belief that it would be a profitable acquisition does not necessarily involve them in liability - this may have been a perfectly proper decision - but the expert's report must state the extent to which the par value of the shares and any premium are to be treated as paid up (a) by the consideration and (b) in cash (s108(4)).

The second problem concerns the declaration of dividends at the end of 1982. Before 1980 the only significant rule was that dividends must not be paid out of capital (*Flitcroft's Case* (1882)), and this allowed the payment of a divdend where there was a surplus on revenue account for the current year even though losses of previous years had not been made good. An unrealised profit generated by a revaluation of fixed assets could also be used to fund a dividend or a bonus issue: *Dimbula Valley* v *Laurie* (1961). New rules were introduced in 1980 (see now CA 1985 Part VIII). Dividends may be paid only out of profits available for the purpose, and the profits available for the purpose are accumulated realised profits less accumulated realised losses so far as not previously written off in a reduction or reorganisation of capital duly made. One very important copnsequence of this is that accounting periods are no longer treated in isolation - thus losses of previous years must be made good before any dividend can be paid. In the case of public companies such as this one there are further restrictions under s264. Plcs may not make distributions if the result would be to reduce the net assets below the sum of the called-up capital and the undistributable reserves (share premium account, capital redemption reserve).

In the present case it is clear that previous losses have not been made good, so that the distribution is unlawful. Under s277 a member who receives a wrongful distribution with actual or constructive knowledge that it is unlawful is liable to repay it to the company. Thus the liquidator could sue for repayment of the dividend.

The third point is the provision of financial assistance to James in respect of the rights issue. It should be observed that the financial assistance here consists not of declaring a dividend but of agreeing to defer the payment for shares. The rules in this area were relaxed somewhat by the 1981 Act (see now CA 1985 ss151-157) but there are still restrictions on what is effectively a disguised return of capital. The general rule is still that it is unlawful for a company or any of its subsidiaries to give assistance for the purchase of that company's shares. There are exceptions if the assistance was not given for the purpose of assisting in the purchase or if it was merely incidental to some broader purpose, but these exceptions (which are couched in regrettably vague and subjective terms) do not appear to apply here. Other exceptions allow the giving of assistance where the directors have made a statutory declaration as to the company's solvency and the transaction has been approved by the General Meeting, but these also are not relevant here.

Breach of s151 is a criminal offence, but there will also be civil liability on James (*Steen* v *Law* (1964)), and the liquidator should therefore be advised that it may be worthwhile bringing an action against James.

7   SHARES

7.1 Introduction

7.2 Key points

7.3 Analysis of questions

7.4 Questions

7.1   Introduction

The subject of shares is a large one, which is in many ways fundamental to the structure and theory of company law; as appears below, some matters related to it are in this book dealt with in other chapters. Students therefore need to be aware that it is not sufficient to be familiar with the material in this chapter, for questions commonly overlap with chapters 6: *Capital and* 11: *Meetings*, as well as occasionally with chapters 12: *Directors* and 13: *Minorities*.

7.2   Key points

a)   *Issuing shares*

Every company must have an authorised capital, and shares may not be issued beyond the limits of that capital.

No shares may be allotted unless the directors have been authorised to allot (CA 1985 s80). Such authority may be given in the Articles or may be conferred by an Ordinary Resolution of the General Meeting. In the latter event it may be valid for a period not exceeding five years.

It is a criminal offence to make an allotment without s80 authority, but this does not affect the validity of the allotment.

In private companies CA 1985 s89 provides that shares issued for cash must initially be offered to existing members in proportion to their shareholdings. A shareholder who suffers loss as a result of a breach of this rule can claim compensation from the company (CA 1985 s95) but the violation does not appear to affect the validity of the allotment.

In all cases the power to issue shares must be exercised bona fide in the best interests of the company. Thus it is not proper to issue shares in order to defeat a motion for the removal of a director, nor to defeat an attempted takeover.

Where it appears that an issue of shares has been made for an improper purpose, the issue can still be ratified by the General Meeting (GM). In such cases the court will order the matter to be referred to the GM for a decision, on the basis that the shares whose issue is disputed may not be voted at that GM.

In addition to the above, the issue of shares for an improper purpose may in some cases be evidence of a course of conduct unfairly oppressive to the minority, so as to bring CA 1985 s459 into consideration. As to this section see chapter 13: *Minorities*.

b)   *Class rights*

Where there are different classes of shares further special problems arise. A modification of the rights attaching to that class of shares normally requires the consent of the holders of the shares of that class at a special meeting as well as a resolution of the GM of the company.

Such resolutions are in any event open to challenge as not having been made in good faith. It is not wholly clear what test is to be applied, but the better view seems to be that the resolution must be for the benefit of holders of that class of shares as a whole. This can cause difficulties where some (but not all) holders of eg preference shares are also holders of ordinary shares, and it is desired to reduce the privileges attaching to the preference shares, thereby benefitting holders of ordinary shares). There have been judicial suggestions that it must be for the benefit of all members of that class including the objectors, but it is thought that this would give too much veto power to a small minority.

c)   *Rules as to payment for shares*

This topic is dealt with in chapter 6: *Capital*.

d)   *Voting rights*

This topic is dealt with in chapter 11: *Meetings*.

e)   *Transfer of shares*

It is common in small private companies for the articles of association to contain restrictions on the freedom to transfer shares. These are considered desirable because of the need to control who becomes a member.

The provisions come in a number of common forms. One form gives the directors an absolute discretion to refuse to register any transfer of shares. A modified version of this removes the discretion where the transfer is to a member of the transferor's family. Another version allows the directors rights of pre-emption on any shares which are to be offered for sale.

Such restrictions are in principle valid, but the power given to the directors must in all cases be exercised bona fide in the best interests of the company.

f)   *Purchase of own shares*

This topic is dealt with in chapter 6: *Capital*.

g)   *Reduction of capital*

This topic is dealt with in chapter 6: *Capital*.

7.3   Analysis of questions

This topic appears quite commonly on London LLB External papers, but often in conjunction with other subjects. This chapter consequently contains a number of cross-references to other chapters.

On the London LLB External Paper these topics have always arisen in the form of problem questions, but it would be perfectly possible to set essay questions in this area, and some examples are included at the end of the chapter.

7.4   Questions

QUESTION 1

The articles of association of Wooden Toys Ltd., give the directors power to issue shares 'in their discretion in such quantities and at such value as they shall determine'. Tim and Bill own 51% of the shares in Wooden Toys Ltd. and they are director. The third and only other director is Jane who owns 10% of the shares. Tim and Bill decide that they will expand the business by buying a company which makes soft toys, despite clear evidence that the soft toy market is shrinking. Jill disagrees with Tim and Bill, believing such expansion to be disastrous. Tim and Bill discover a very successful firm making teddy bears but as Wooden Toys Ltd. lacks sufficient capital to make an immediate bid for the teddy bear firm, Tim and Bill issue shares which they place with known supporters to raise capital. This also has the effect of reducing Jill's voting power. They then call a general meeting at which they pass a resolution to dismiss Jill as a director. They and their supporters also pass a special resolution deleting the provision in the articles in terms of which she would have been entitled to compensation, and requiring her to sell her shares.

Advise Jill.

University of London LLB Examination
(for External Students) Company Law June 1986 Q6

General comment

The first question in this chapter concentrates on the matters listed under (a) above. These are always likely to arise together, since all of them can very easily be relevant on the same set of facts. It should be observed that this question is really mainly about the rights attaching to shares although it is posed in the context of the attempted removal of a director.

Skeleton solution

Articles contain s80 authority - apparently not revoked - allotment probably valid.

Power to issue shares must be exercised for proper purpose - Jill may be able to challenge on this basis.

Note s459 and IA s122 - these remedies are probably too drastic for the present case.

Suggested solution

Jill is a minority shareholder and a director in the company. She is concerned about the issue of shares to Tim and Bill. It appears that the Articles give the directors s80 authority, and that they can therefore issue shares freely. The authority could have been revoked by an Ordinary Resolution, but this has not been done (and Jill could not have done it by herself anyway, since she is a minority shareholder). Thus it seems that the allotment does not violate s80.

However, there are other restrictions on the allotment of shares. The directors' power to issue shares is a fiduciary one and must be used for a proper purpose. Defeating a take-over bid or maintaining the directors' own position are not proper purposes - *Howard Smith Ltd* v *Ampol Petroleum Ltd* (1973), *Hogg* v *Cramphorn* (1967) - and Jill may well be able to challenge the allotment on that basis. If the matter appears doubtful when considered by the court, it may be submitted by the court to a General Meeting of the company to decide, the shares under dispute not being allowed to vote at that meeting. Again, this will not help Jill, for she is already a minority shareholder and her opponents will be able to pass the Ordinary Resolution necessary to approve the allotment of the new shares.

Companies Act (CA) ss89-96 are also relevant here. These give existing shareholders rights of pre-emption when new shares are issued. If the new shares are offered for cash, then they must be offered to existing shareholders in proportion to their present holdings. This does not seem to have happened here, for the shares have simply been allotted to the friends of Tim and Bill. Under CA 1985 s95 the company, as well as Tim and Bill, are liable to compensate Jill for loss, damage, costs or expenses incurred. The Act gives no right to challenge the validity of the allotment, and it is generally believed that no such right can exist independently of the statute. It is unclear whether the statutory right to compensation includes loss of profits and/or influence in the company.

Jill may also wish to complain of her removal as a director. Under s303 a director may always be removed by Ordinary Resolution, but this is without prejudice to the right to claim damages for wrongful and/or unfair dismissal. In order to succeed in these claims Jill will have to show that there was a contract of service between her and the company. From the question it seems that the arrangements for her employment were contained in the Articles, and only with the security provided therein: *Re New British Iron Co* (1898), *Read* v *Astoria Garage (Streatham) Ltd* (1952). It also seems that she would have been entitled to compensation but for the change in the articles. She therefore needs to challenge the validity of the resolution to change the Articles.

Jill is a shareholder and as such has locus standi to challenge the resolution on the grounds that it was not passed bona fide for the benefit of the company as a whole. There are really two motions in the one resolution, but it is thought that this is legally permissible, if practically undesirable. In *Greenhalgh* v *Arderne Cinemas* (1946) it was said that the test for whether a resolution is passed for the benefit of the company as a whole is whether it is for the benefit of a hypothetical individual shareholder. The difficulty with this approach is that the hypothetical individual shareholder by definition does not exist, and the test is inappropriate in the context of a majority and minority who are at odds with each other. In *Clemens* v *Clemens* (1976) Foster J substituted the actual aggrieved member for the hypothetical member, but this test seems to go much too far, for it is unlikely that any complaint would be made by an individual member if the resolution was for his benefit; consequently the test comes close to giving the minority a right of veto on matters which are supposed to be decided by Ordinary Resolution.

An alternative test suggested in *Greenhalgh* v *Arderne Cinemas* (1946) was whether the resolution discriminates between the majority and the minority. It is submitted that this test should not be taken too far. Where a resolution does so discriminate, this may well be evidence of an improper purpose in passing it, but it cannot be conclusive. Here, though, it seems most unlikely that the majority can find a legitimate explanation for acting as they have done.

The conclusion of the above must be that Jill can claim compensation for removal under s303 (provided of course that her contract of service has been duly approved under s319).

In the next question an unusual, but perfectly plausible, combination of issues occurs. The question of issuing new shares is combined with that of capital reduction. This question overlaps considerably between Chapter 6 and Chapter 7, but is dealt with here for convenience.

QUESTION 2

The share capital of Adventure Games Ltd. ('the company') consists of £500,000 divided into 400,000 £1 ordinary shares and £100,000 £1 6% preference shares. The preference shares also have the right to priority in the repayment of capital and limited participation rights £1 per share out of any surplus on a winding up. The preference shares are also fully participating as to dividends. The directors of the company felt that the preference shares represented a substantial obstacle to the future prosperity of the company and tried to negotiate terms for the repayment of capital to the preference shareholders and their elimination from the company, but it was clear that an overwhelming number of preference shareholders would reject this. The directors now ask you whether either of the following schemes might work:

Scheme 1:

They would issue a further 300,000 shares with identical rights to the existing preference shares, and allot these to members sympathetic to their aims; and they would call a class meeting of preference shareholders which would then vote in favour of the directors' proposal for repayment.

Scheme 2:

They would cause the company to pass a special resolution reducing the company's capital by 20% in accordance with a scheme in terms of which the preference shareholders were to be repaid the full nominal value of their shares and were to be eliminated as shareholders.

Advise the directors.

University of London LLB Examination
(for External Students) Company Law June 1986 Q7

Skeleton solution

All shares rank equally unless divided into classes. Scheme 1 requires authority in GM, which can probably be obtained. Pre-emption rights do not apply. The allotment can be challenged for want of bona fides. As some preference shareholders are also ordinary shareholders, Scheme 1 may well be ruled unlawful.

Scheme 2 is a reduction of capital. Interests of creditors, shareholders and public at large must be considered. Here the difficulty is that class rights of preference shareholders may not be adequately protected. Scheme 2 may need to be modified.

Suggested solution

An ordinary share carries rights of attendance and voting at meetings, together with dividends and return of capital in the event of a winding-up. A preference share normally carries certain preferential rights in respect of these matters, but does not normally carry a right to vote at general meetings. Prima facie all shares rank equally (*Birch* v *Cropper* (1889)), but once they have been divided into classes (as is commonly done in large companies) the rights stated as attaching to shares of a particular class are exhaustive: *Isle of Wight* v *Tahourdin* (1883); *Scottish Insurance Corporation Ltd* v *Wilsons & Clyde Coal Co Ltd* (1949).

The directors propose to issue a further 300,000 shares with identical rights to the existing shareholders so that the consent of the class to Scheme 1 can be obtained. Authority under Companies Act (CA) s80 is required for the allotment of shares, and this can be obtained either through the articles or by means of an Ordinary Resolution of the company. In the present case it seems that the latter will be required. It may be noted that the authority given cannot exceed five years. Here there will be no apparent problem in securing the passage of the Resolution, but the directors will need to be aware that an allotment of shares must be made for a proper purpose - otherwise it is liable to be set aside by the court (*Hogg* v *Cramphorn* (1967), *Howard Smith* v *Ampol* (1973)), though it can subsequently be ratified by the General Meeting, and it seems likely that this would happen here. The statutory pre-emption rights under CA ss89-96 are not applicable, because these preference shares are not 'relevant shares' within s94(5).

The major problem for the directors would be the validity or otherwise of a resolution passed at a class meeting of the preference shareholders. The test is that laid down in *Allen* v *Gold Reefs of West Africa* (1900), namely whether the resolution is passed bona fide for the benefit of the class as a whole. The consent of the preference shareholders is required under CA s125(2) since the Scheme involves a variation of their rights (though it is to be noted that the issue of the new shares is not a variation of their rights, but merely a variation of the value and enjoyment of those rights: *White* v *Bristol Aeroplane Co* (1953); *Greenhalgh* v *Arderne Cinemas* (1946).

In the present case a difficulty arises because some of the preference shareholders are also ordinary shareholders, and it is submitted that the resolution of the class meeting would be open to challenge because it appears that those voting in favour of the resolution have done so in order to benefit themselves as ordinary shareholders rather than to benefit the preference shareholders as a class (cf *Re Holders Investment Trust* (1971)).

It is therefore thought that Scheme 1 is unlikely to survive a challenge.

Scheme 2 would perhaps be preferable. It is a straightforward reduction of capital under s135, requiring the passage of a special resolution and confirmation by the court. Generally the court is pre-disposed to grant such confirmation so long as the interests of creditors are adequately protected: *Poole* v *National Bank of China* (1907). The interests of the shareholders are considered next, followed by the interests of the public at large: *ex parte Westburn Sugar Refineries* (1951). In practice it is rare for confirmation to be refused, and a Scottish judge (Lord Cooper) has gone so far as to describe the confirmation procedure as a 'rubber stamp': *Scottish Insurance* v *Wilsons & Clyde Coal Co* (1949).

In the present case it looks as if the real objection will come from the preference shareholders. The general rule in such cases is that the shareholders must be treated according to the rights they would enjoy on a winding-up: *Scottish Insurance* v *Wilsons & Clyde Coal Co*. It may be that a reduction does not involve a variation of rights, and it may produce great unfairness, as in *Re Mackenzie* (1916) where the preference shareholders were obliged to give up a large fraction of their annual dividend, whilst the ordinary shareholders sacrificed nothing.

If the preference shareholders are treated in accordance with their class rights then the reduction will not involve any variation of rights (*Re Saltdean Estate Co Ltd* (1968)) and the reduction will be confirmed as a matter of course. However, if the shareholders' rights are not respected there is a risk that confirmation will be refused; there are only two reported cases this century where shareholders' objections have led to the refusal of confirmation - *Re Old Silkstone Collieries* (1954) and *Re Holder's Investment Trust* (1971) - and in both cases the reason was that class rights had not been respected. In such cases it appears that confirmation may still be given if the court can be persuaded that the scheme is fair, but this is a very heavy burden to discharge where class rights are not being respected.

It is therefore thought that Scheme 2 will require some modification before there is a reasonable prospect of obtaining the court's approval.

Finally, it may be worth advising the directors of the possibility of using the provisions for re-purchase of shares under ss162-164. The articles would have to altered to give a power to purchase the shares and a Special Resolution would then have to be passed to authorise an off-market purchase.

QUESTION 3

'The restrictions on the issue of new shares by a private company are an unjustified fetter on the freedom to raise capital.' Discuss.

Written by Editor
September 1989

General comment

The final question in this chapter is not taken from a London LLB External paper, but is included to provide an example of an essay question on the issue of new shares. It may be noted that this question is the only one in this chapter to deal with the rather neglected question of the effect of exceeding authorised capital, a point which could easily be raised in a problem question.

Skeleton solution

Three restrictions: authorised capital, directors' authority, pre-emption rights.

Authorised capital: easily increased, no authority on effect of accidentally exceeding it. Issue possibly void.

Directors' authority: gives shareholders some control, issue without authority valid, but criminal offence by directors.

Pre-emption rights: protects existing shareholders, damages for breach, unclear whether allotment invalid.

Rules try to balance power between directors and shareholders: they impose some constraints at company's freedom, but these are basically justified.

Suggested solution

A private company which wishes to issue new shares must be careful to comply with three major requirements, two of which did not exist before 1980. These are the limit of authorised capital, the requirement that the directors be authorised to issue new shares and the pre-emption rights of existing shareholders.

Authorised capital: A company is required to have an authorised capital, which must be stated in the memorandum (Companies Act (CA) 1985 s2). This capital can be increased by Ordinary Resolution, which must be filed with the Registrar within 15 days (s121). The Act is silent on the question of what happens where shares are issued in excess of the authorised capital. There is of course no good reason why this should happen, since authority for an increase can so easily be obtained, but it might occur by oversight. It is generally thought that such an issue would be void since the shares do not properly exist, but there is no authority on the point, and it is not impossible that a court would seek to avoid this very awkward conclusion.

Directors' authority: CA 1985 s80 requires directors to have authority before allotting any shares in the company. Such authority may be contained in the articles, or may be given (for a period of up to five years) by Ordinary Resolution of the company. An issue of shares made in violation of this requirement is a criminal offence by the directors and anyone else who is knowingly a party to it, but this does not affect the validity of the allotment.

Pre-emption rights: CA 1985 s89 requires shares issued for cash to be offered to existing shareholders pro rata to their existing holdings before being offered elsewhere. Section 92 allows a shareholder whose pre-emption rights are ignored to claim damages from the company, but there is no provision which expressly invalidates the allotment, and it is thought (again in the absence of any authority) that it would be valid.

In addition to the above directors need to be aware that an allotment which is made for an improper purpose, such as to benefit the directors personally, or to defeat a take-over bid is liable to be set aside, or at least referred to a General Meeting of the company: *Hogg* v *Cramphorn* (1967); *Howard Smith* v *Ampol* (1973).

It is fair to say that the legal restrictions, especially the s80 authority and the pre-emption rights, were introduced to protect existing shareholders from having their shareholdings diluted or the value of them weakened by an unnecessary issue of shares. Of course it may be argued that the 'proper purposes' doctrine serves much the same purpose, so that the statutory rules are unnecessary. However, it is to be observed that the test of what is a proper purpose is inevitably imprecise. The statutory rules have the merit of clarity and certainty. At the same time it must be admitted that they do add some additional bureaucracy to the process of issuing shares; it is nevertheless submitted that they are on balance to be welcomed as a useful protection for minority shareholders.

8   DEBENTURES

8.1 Introduction

8.2 Key points

8.3 Recent cases and statutes

8.4 Analysis of questions

8.5 Questions

8.1   Introduction

This chapter examines the problems which arise in connection with the taking of loans by a company in return for a debenture, the document evidencing the indebtedness, which will most commonly be secured in some way on the assets of the company.

8.2   Key points

a) *Debentures*

A debenture is a document by which a company acknowledges its indebtedness under a loan. The loan will normally be secured on the assets of the company, either on specific assets - usually a building - in which case it is a fixed charge, or on the assets of the company from time to time, in which case it is a floating charge.

The major difficulties in this area arise in deciding when floating charges become enforceable, and in dealing with the priorities between a number of different charges.

b) *Registration*

A debenture needs to be registered at the Companies Registry within twenty-one days of its creation. Failure to comply with this requirement renders the security void, though it does not invalidate the loan.

c) *Fixed and floating charges*

A fixed charge attaches to specific assets of the company, whereas a floating charge is applicable to the assets for the time being. It is inherent in the notion of a floating charge that the assets which are subject to it can be freely bought and sold as part of the company's business. This state of affairs ceases if the charge 'crystalises', which will happen if the payments due on the debenture are not properly made or if the company goes into liquidation; thereafter the charge attaches to the assets of the comany at that date, which may not be dealt with without the consent of the debenture holder.

Fixed charges are likely to be mortgages for the purposes of land law. According to whether or not the land is registered, it may be necessary to register the mortgage at the Land Registry or the Land Charges Registry.

Fixed chargees rank above floating chargees in the order of priority in a liquidation.

d) *Automatic crystallisation*

Floating chargees frequently seek to protect themselves against the risk of the subsequent creation of fixed charges which would rank in priority to their own floating charges. To this end clauses are commonly inserted in floating charges providing that on the creation of any such fixed charge the floating charge will automatically and immediately crystallise. It has become a question of some controversy whether such clauses are legally valid. There are dicta in *Davey* v *Williamson* [1898] 2 QB 194 and in *Evans* v *Rival Granite Quarries Ltd* [1910] 2 KB 979 which support the validity of such clauses, and the idea was canvassed again more recently by Hoffmann J in *Re Brightlife Ltd* [1986] BCLC 418, but there is no English case in which it has been definitively held that the clauses are valid. In New Zealand *Re Manurewa* [1971] NZLR 909 clearly upholds such clauses. The policy objection to clauses of this kind is that they subvert the principle that fixed charges take precedence over floating charges, but at the present time it is unclear what view the courts will eventually take.

e) *Restrictive clauses*

Related to the above point is the concept of a restrictive clause. This is a clause which seeks to forbid the later creation of charges ranking in priority, not by means of automatic crystallisation but simply by making the subsequent charge ineffective. The difficulty is that this seeks to affect the validity of one contract by means of a clause in another contract, which is clearly contrary to principles of privity of contract. Because of this the English courts have generally been hostile to rectrictive clauses. The present position is that such a clause is effective only if it can be shown that the later chargee has actual knowledge of both the existence of the earlier charge and the inclusion in it of the restrictive clause. The constructive knowledge provided by registration of the charge is not sufficient for this purpose - *Re Castell and Brown* [1898] 1 Ch 315, *Wilson* v *Kelland* [1910] 2 Ch 30.

f) *Multiple floating charges*

More than one floating charge may be created by the same company. In this event it is virtually inevitable that the same assets will be subject to multiple charges. As between floating charges the general rule is that the first in time of registration prevails.

8.3   Recent cases and statutes

It should be noted that the Companies Act 1989 has made important changes in the law relating to the registration of company charges, an area on which problem

problem questions are frequently set.

8.4 Analysis of questions

Debentures have been a consistently popular topic on the London LLB External paper, occurring every year since 1983, and consequently represent a sensible choice of subject for students preparing for that examination. Debentures commonly occur in connection with liquidation (since it is usually only then that questions about the validity of the debenture come to the fore). Consequently, the subject-matter of this chapter overlaps to some extent with that of chapter 10: *Liquidations* to which reference should also be made. However, this chapter contains a good deal of material which is relevant to the procedure to be followed in liquidations where the company has granted debentures.

Generally it may be said that the major points raised in these questions are: priorities between charges (especially where one charge is fixed and another floating) clauses restricting the power to create later charges and automatic crystallisation clauses. The position of preferential creditors in a liquidation is often thrown in as a minor point.

8.5 Questions

QUESTION 1

Tessa is the managing director of Gorgeous Garments Ltd ('the company'). The nominal capital of the company is £100,000 divided into £1 shares, of which 20,000 have been issued - the bulk to Tessa - and are fully paid. The company has an outstanding loan for £50,000 with the West Bank, which loan has been personally guaranteed by Tessa. After a few years of quite successful trading in the 1970s the market in the clothes manufactured by the company slumped and the West Bank became worried about their loan. Tessa realised that if the loan were called in, the company might have to go into liquidation, and therefore devised the following scheme:

1.   She arranged for the company to borrow £50,000 from the Metropolitan Bank Ltd, which loan was evidenced by a debenture and secured by a floating charge on all the company's undertaking, executed on 30th January 1982.

2.   She persuaded the West Bank not to call in the outstanding loan, on the condition that half was repaid and the remainder secured by a floating charge on the company's book debts. It was agreed, however, that this would be done by the company making a prepayment in full of the £50,000 loan and a subsequent loan of £25,000 made by the West Bank to the company. On this basis a debenture and floating charge were executed in favour of the West Bank on the 2nd February 1982 and a document was signed formally releasing Tessa from her personal guarantee.

Both these charges were registered on the 18th February 1982. With the market even more depressed, Tessa, in a desperate attempt to stave off liquidation, ordered 100,000 blouses from Hong Kong in the hope that she might sell them at a quick profit. This only made matters worse and from June 1982 the company was only able to pay

Margaret, the secretary, £250 per month, half her monthly salary. Finally in December, Margaret presented a petition for the winding up of the company and an order to this effect was eventually granted in March 1983.

When all the company's assets have been sold the liquidator will have little more than £5,000 to meet all the creditors' claims.

Discuss.

University of London LLB Examination
(for External Students) Company Law June 1983 Q7

General comment

This question concentrates on the order of payment in liquidations, but candidates are also expected to consider Tessa's possible personal liability.

Skeleton solution

Liquidations retrospective to date of petition. IA s245 probably catches West Bank Scheme. Fradulent and wrongful trading also relevant, though fraud is hard to prove.

Between floating charges first in line prevails except where one is specific order of payment: costs, preferential creditors, West Bank, Met Bank.

Suggested solution

In a liquidation money must be paid out in a strict order of priority. The first payment is the costs and expenses of the liquidation, then the fixed chargees, then the preferential creditors, then the floating chargees. Next come the unsecured trade creditors, followed by the preference and ordinary shareholders. In some cases it is also necessary to take into account such matters as distraint, enforcement of liens and Romalpa clauses, but these points do not appear in the present question.

The liquidator should also bear in mind ss212-214 and 245 Insolvency Act 1986.

The liquidation is deemed to have commenced on the date of the petition, ie December 1982. Under s245 the granting of a floating charge or a payment by a company within six months of the commencement of the winding up will be void if made at a time when the company was insolvent, except to the extent that fresh consideration was provided for it. This section would appear to catch the scheme entered into with the West Bank (though not the loan from the Metropolitan Bank), though it is not wholly clear whether the company was insolvent immediately after entering into this transaction. Insolvency Act ss213, 214 are also relevant. A director of a company incurs personal liability for 'wrongful trading' ie continuing to trade knowing that the company is insolvent. Any person may incur personal liability for 'fraudulent trading', ie trading in such a way as fraudulently to prefer one creditor as against another. There must be a considerable risk in the present case that Teresa will find herself liable under both these provisions. Under the statutory predecessors of these provisions a narrow view was taken of the concepts of 'defraud' and 'fraudulent purpose' (*Re Patrick and Lyon* (1933)) but it should not be assumed that the same approach would be taken at the present day, as attitudes to wrongdoing by directors seem to have hardened somewhat.

Assuming that neither charge is invalidated by any of the statutory provisions, it remains to be seen how the liquidator might deal with competing charges. Both are floating charges and the usual rule is that the second cannot take priority over the first, at least where both are general charges over all the assets of the business: *Re Benjamin Cope* (1914). However, this rule need not apply where one charge is a general one and the other is specific to particular property: *Re Automatic Bottlemakers* (1926). Thus in this case it is possible for West Bank's charge to take in priority.

In summary, the liquidator should be advised that the first payment out is the costs and expenses of the liquidation. The second payment is to the preferential creditors (including Margaret's salary for the previous four months up to a maximum of £800), then come the West Bank's charge and finally Metropolitan Bank's charge to the extent that these are not invalidated.

QUESTION 2

Honest Brokers Ltd had an overdraft with its Bank, West Bank plc, for £100,000 until it was told by the manager that it must either reduce the overdraft or provide security. Consequently in January 1983 Honest Brokers executed a floating charge in favour of West Bank over all its undertaking to secure all sums then owing and any further sums borrowed in the future. The floating charge also provided that no other charges, fixed or floating which might have priority to or rank pari passu with it, would be issued by Honest Brokers without the written permission of West Bank. It also provided that on the issue of any compulsory process against Honest Brokers, the floating charge would immediately crystallise. In May 1983, despite these provisions, Honest Brokers borrowed £50,000 from the North Bank plc, and deposited with the North Bank the title deeds to a house owned by Honest Brokers. Between January and June 1983, Honest Brokers paid in £100,000 into its account with West Bank, but also drew out the same amount. In June 1983, Charles, the secretary of Honest Brokers, who had received only half his monthly salary (£250 instead of £500) for the past six months presented a petition for the winding up of the company, and despite protracted negotiations to save the company, a winding-up order was granted in February 1984.

Advise the liquidators.

University of London LLB Examination
(for External Students) Company Law June 1984 Q7

General comment

This is a more complex question on the same area as Question 1. It adds in problems relating to clauses restricting the right to create further charges.

Skeleton solution

Distinguish fixed and floating charges - concept of crystallisation - fixed charge to

North Bank takes priority unless caught by negative pledge and automatic crystallisation clause. This happens only if later chargee has actual notice of earlier clauses. Validity of automative crystallisation clauses now seems accepted after some earlier uncertainty.

IA s245 may invalidate the floating charge, but this is unclear.

Suggested solution

A debenture is a document evidencing a debt that the company owes, and it may be secured or unsecured. Security is usually by way of a fixed or floating charge. A fixed charge may be legal or equitable (*Re Castell and Brown* (1898)) but a floating charge is necessarily equitable and generally possesses three characteristics; it is a charge on the assets of a company, present and future, that class of assets being one which would in the ordinary course of business change, and until some future step is taken the company is free to carry on business in the normal way: *Re Yorkshire Woolcombers Association Ltd* (1904). When the charge ceases to float and instead becomes fixed, it is said to crystallise - this normally only occurs on the appointment of a receiver or the commencement of a winding-up.

The liquidators will be concerned to establish the priority of payments to be made in the liquidation. In January 1983 Honest Brokers Ltd executed a floating charge in favour of West Bank Ltd with a restrictive clause and an automatic crystallisation clause. In May 1983 Honest Brokers Ltd deposited title deeds with North Bank Ltd to secure further borrowings. The latter charge is an equitable fixed charge and will take in priority to the floating charge unless it is caught by the restrictive clause.

A restrictive clause attempts to prevent a company from engaging in particular kinds of transactions, especially the creation of later charges which may rank in priority to the existing floating charge. The problem is that the floating charge leaves a company with the freedom to deal with its assets as it pleases, including creating charges over them, unless some provision can be inserted to prevent this. Such clauses are in principle valid, but are likely to be construed strictly: *Robson* v *Smith* (1895); *Cox* v *Dublin Distillery* (1906). The fear of the floating chargee is that the company will later create a fixed charge which on the normal rules of priority will have to be paid back first.

In *Re Castell and Brown* an equitable fixed charge created by a deposit of title deeds took in priority to a previous floating charge. To bind the later fixed chargee, it is necessary that the latter should have notice of the existence of the previous charge and notice of the restrictive clause. When the floating charge in favour of WB Ltd is registered this gives notice of its existence but not of its terms: *Wilson* v *Kelland* (1910). This is an old case which was decided before restrictive clauses were common, but it remains good law; thus the North Bank must be actually informed of the restrictive clause at the time of the deposit of title deeds, and this has not been done. In *Siebe Gorman* v *Barclays Bank Ltd* (1979) there is support for the view that such clauses are so common at the present day that knowledge should be inferred, but in general the cases do not go to this length.

Thus the charge in favour of North Bank would take in priority to that in favour of West Bank because there was no communicated notice of the restrictive clause. The question then is whether the Automatic Crystallisation Clause (ACC) makes any difference. The charge in favour of West Bank is to crystallise on the issue of compulsory process (eg the June 1983 winding-up petition.) It is clear law that a floating charge becomes fixed when a receiver is appointed or when a winding-up is commenced. It is much less clear whether crystallisation can happen automatically, ie on the happening of some defined event. There are dicta to this effect in *Government Stock* v *Manila Railways* (1897), *Evans* v *Rival Granite* (1910) and *Davey & Co* v *Williamson* (1898), but there are also serious policy objections to the concept. In *Re Manurewa* (1971) (a New Zealand case) the ACC was dependent on breach of a restrictive clause and was held to be valid although it involved crystallisation without the business coming to an end. The policy objections are that it may be difficult to establish exactly when crystallisation occurs and the fact that it may well occur without third parties realising, so that they may lend money to the company without being aware that a fixed charge exists.

At present the law in this area is unclear, though the decision of Hoffmann J in *Re Brightlife* (1986) provides some evidence that ACCs are becoming accepted in English law. Even if the ACC is valid, this would not affect the priority between the two charges.

Insolvency Act 1986 s245 must also be considered in relation to the floating charge (it does not apply to fixed charges). It provides that a floating charge created within twelve months of the presentation of a winding-up petition is invalid if the company was insolvent immediately after the creation of the charge except to the extent that fresh consideration was given for the creation of the charge (in other words such a charge cannot be used to secure pre-existing borrowings). In the present case the company was insolvent when the charge was created, so it is necessary to look for fresh consideration. In line with the decision in *Re Yeovil Glove Co Ltd* (1965) and the rule in *Clayton's case* (1816) it is arguable that the bank here did advance fresh consideration, so that s245 does not operate to invalidate the charge.

Thus the payments out in the liquidation are (in order): costs and expenses of the liquidation, the equitable fixed charge, the preferential creditors (including Charles's wages in the previous four months, the floating charge, the unsecured creditors.

QUESTION 3

Bandwagon Ltd owed £100,000 to its bank, which debt was personally guaranteed by Harry, its majority shareholder and managing director. Harry became worried about the company's prospects, and since it was very short of cash, in February 1984, he made a loan of £100,000 to it, which loan was evidenced by a debenture and secured by a floating charge over the company's entire undertaking. The charge included a provision that if the company gave any further charges or suffered any enforcement proceedings, the charge would be deemed to have crystallised the moment before any such further charge or before any judgment given in any enforcement proceedings. This restrictive clause was registered together with all other particulars within the prescribed time limit under the provisions of s95 of the Companies Act 1948.

In April 1984, the company repaid half the debt to its bank. In May 1984, the company borrowed £50,000 from Roger and secured this debt by depositing with Roger the title deeds to its factory.

He is responsible for the statement in the prospectus that 'when planning permission is granted this will be a prime site for the proposed development'. The prospectus further states that Bill, Harold and Jane will become directors of Terco plc and describes them as specialists in the field. None have any formal qualifications, Bill and Jane become directors but Harold suffers a heart attack and declines to become a director on health grounds. Albert acquires 1,000 shares in the company. The company fails to get permission for Roger failed to check the register and was therefore unaware of the restrictive clause in the company's earlier charge given to Harry. Thereafter the company paid off the rest of its overdraft and in a desperate attempt to stave off an insolvent liquidation made a number of wild speculations which all failed.

In February 1985, Basil, the company's secretary, who for the previous 6 months had only been paid half his salary, presented a petition for the winding up of the company and an order was granted on this petition in May 1985.

Advise the liquidator how to deal with the respective claims of Harry, Roger, Basil and unsecured creditors with claims totalling well over £50,000, bearing in mind that the company's assets are no more than £10,000.

University of London LLB Examination
(for External Students) Company Law June 1985 Q4

General comment

Another question on very similar lines to those above.

Skeleton solution

R has fixed charge. H may have charge which became fixed just before R's charge. If H's charge still floating, R has priority. Question is whether automatic crystallisation clause is effective, and the position is unclear. Note also that IA s245 may invalidate the later charge.

Suggested solution

In a liquidation the first payment is of the costs and expenses of the liquidation; thereafter the fixed chargees will be paid.

It is clear that Roger has an equitable fixed charge, since such a charge arises on the deposit of title deeds: *Re Castell & Brown* (1898). This was created in May 1984 (and it is assumed that it was duly registered within 21 days) and the liquidation commenced in February 1985. However, there is a possibility that Harry has priority over Roger, because it is arguable that the former's floating charge became a fixed charge through breach of the restrictive clause just before the creation of Roger's charge.

Thus it is necessary to advise the liquidator on priorities as affected by restrictive clauses and automatic crystallisation clauses. A further complication arises if Harry's charge is invalidated by Insolvency Act (IA) 1986 s245 (as to this see below).

In general a fixed charge takes priority over a floating charge. This is so even when the floating charge was the first in time, unless the fixed chargee had notice of the floating charge and the restrictive clause when the fixed charge was created. Registration gives constructive notice of the former but not of the latter: *Wilson* v *Kelland* (1910). A restrictive clause fetters the company's power to deal with its assets, and is thus on the face of it incompatible with the notion of a floating charge. Despite this such clauses are valid, but they are also strictly construed: *Cox* v *Dublin Distillery* (1906); *Robson* v *Smith* (1895).

Thus here the vital question is whether Harry's charge was floating or fixed as at May 1984. If fixed, it would take priority over Roger, since the first in time rule would then apply. Roger is apparently under no duty to search the Register, even though clauses of this kind are very common at the present day.

The question refers to the clause as a restrictive clause, but it is really just an automatic crystallisation clause, since it attempts to state what will be the consequences if another charge is created.

The general concept of a floating charge was explained in *Re Yorkshire Woolcombers* (1904) as a charge over assets present and future, those being assets which would in the ordinary course of business change, the charge to remain floating until some event occurs which causes crystallisation. The events which are normally regarding as causing crystallisation are the appointment of a receiver and the commencement of a winding-up: *Re Victoria Steamboats* (1897). The difficulty is to decide on the validity of express clauses which make crystallisation happen on the occurrence of other specified events, ie automatic crystallisation clauses. The point does not seem to be settled in English law, but the general view seems to be that the business must be at an end, either through receivership or liquidation (*Re Florence Land and Public Works Co* (1878)) or because it has come to a natural end so that it is not worth appointing anyone to wind it up: *Evans* v *Rival Granite* (1910); *Government Stock* v *Manila Railway Co* (1897); *Davey & Co* v *Williamson* (1898).

In the New Zealand case of *Re Manurewa* (1971) crystallisation was to take place automatically on breach of the restrictive clause, and the court accepted that this provision was valid and effective. However, the English courts seem to have been more influenced by the argument that the adoption of such a scheme might be unfair on other creditors (including future creditors) who could advance money without being aware that an earlier floating charge had crystallised. On this basis it seems that Roger would take in priority to Harry. Attention is drawn, however, to the decision of Hoffmann J in *Re Brightlife* (1986), which evidences some support for the recognition of these clauses in English law.

In any event there is the possibility that Harry's charge is invalidated by IA 1986 s245. This provides that where in the twelve months before the commencement of a winding-up a floating charge is created and the company was insolvent immediately after the creation, the charge will be invalid except to the extent that fresh consideration was given for it. It seems probable that the company was insolvent, but fresh consideration of £100,000 has been advanced, so to that extent the charge will apparently be valid. The one difficulty with this argument is that the 'fresh' consideration is arguably not fresh at all, but merely the re-financing of the company's debts so as to relieve Harry's liability under the guarantees which he gave. If this argument is accepted, then s245 will apply, and the charge will be invalidated.

The liquidator should be advised to pay Roger first, then the preferential creditors (including Basil's unpaid wages in the four months preceding the liquidation, the Inland Revenue, DSS and others). Then, if Harry's charge is valid, he should be paid ahead of the ordinary trade creditors.

QUESTION 4

Arrivals and Departures Ltd. ('the company') operated a delivery and removal service. It had a paid up share capital of £100 of which Harry owned 99 in his own name, with the other share being held on trust for him. The operations of the company were financed by a bank overdraft with the Midweek Bank. In 1985, when the overdraft stood at £50,000 the bank demanded security and the company executed a floating charge over all its undertaking to secure the amount outstanding and 'any subsequent amounts' loaned by the bank to the company. This charge contained a clause prohibiting the creation of any subsequent charges having priority over it or ranking pari passu with it. It also contained a clause to the effect that it would crystallise automatically if any enforcement or forfeiture proceedings were taken against the company. This charge was executed on 1 May 1985 and registered on 15 May 1985.

Between May and December the company continue trading, having a turnover of £100,000. It then got into difficulties and when it was unable to pay a lorry repair bill, the garage which carried out the repair - Mobile Motors - asserted a lien over the lorry. A week later, on 1 March 1986, Benjamin, an employee who was owed £5,000 in salary arrears presented a petition for the winding up of the company. There were protracted negotiations to save the company, but they failed and on 28 May 1986, a winding up order was granted. The assets amount to about £10,000.

Discuss the order of priority in which the claims by Midweek Bank (the overdraft on liquidation was £120,000), Mobile Motors and Benjamin are to be met.

University of London LLB Examination
(for External Students) Company Law June 1986 Q4

Skeleton solution

Liquidation is retrospective to date of petition. Definition of floating charge. M Bank will rely on automatic crystallisation clause to defeat the lien, but the validity of these in English law is unsettled. If charge still floating, IA s245 may partially invalidate it. B is a preferential creditor. Order of payment is: costs, lien, B, floating charge, unsecured creditors.

Suggested solution

The company entered liquidation on 1st March 1986, since it is the date of presentation of the petition which is the crucial date.

A debenture is a document evidencing the company's indebtedness, which is usually secured by a fixed and/or floating charge. Here a floating charge has been issued; this was defined by Romer LJ in *Re Yorkshire Woolcombers* (1904) as possessing the following three characteristics: first, it is a charge over assets present and future, second those assets would in the ordinary course of business change, third the charge continues to float unless and until some event causes it to crystallise; until that time the company is free to deal with the assets which are subject to the floating charge. This last point is a great practical advantage to the company, but it may be necessary for the creditor to act promptly if his security appears to be in danger. In an effort to gain extra protection the holders of floating charges began to insert in them restrictive clauses forbidding the company to create later charges which ranked in priority to the earlier ones. Such clauses are valid, but are construed strictly (*Robson v Smith* (1895)) but their effectiveness as against the holders of later fixed charges depends upon those holders having actual notice of the earlier charge and the restrictive clause. Registration under s395 gives constructive notice of the former but not of the latter: *Wilson v Kelland* (1910).

Midweek Bank has a floating charge with a restrictive clause in it, but this has not prevented a lien from arising in favour of Mobile Motors. This is a major problem with such clauses, for the debenture holder has no practical remedy to make good the breach when liquidation follows. Midweek Bank would like to claim that the charge had crystallised before the lien arose, so that it would rank above the lien, which it would not otherwise do. The success of this argument depends upon whether automatic crystallisation clauses are valid. It is settled that crystallisation happens on the appointment of a receiver or the commencement of a winding-up, and there is authority to suggest that the same happens where the business ceases to be a going concern: *Davey v Williamson* (1898); *Evans v Rival Granite* (1910); *Re Woodroffes (Musical Instruments) Ltd* (1985). However, English law has traditionally been hostile to automatic crystallisation clauses like the one encountered here. The policy objection to this solution, namely that a floating charge may become fixed without any current or later creditors being aware of the fact seems to have prevailed, though in *Re Brightlife* (1986) Hoffmann J showed rather more sympathy for these clauses than has been usual. The position is better settled in New Zealand where *Re Manurewa* (1971) is authority for the validity of automatic crystallisation clauses. This case is of no more than persuasive authority in this country, and it is suggested that it will not be followed here.

If the charge is still a floating charge, then it is necessary to consider Insolvency Act 1986 s245; the charge was granted within the twelve months prior to liquidation, but the Bank appears to have advanced cash after the charge was granted. It will thus be a secured creditor for £50,000, but unsecured for the rest.

Benjamin is entitled to preferential treatment in respect of unpaid wages in the four months preceding 1st March 1986 up to a maximum of £800. He ranks below the costs of the liquidation and the lien, but above the floating charge. The unsecured trade creditors rank after the floating charge.

QUESTION 5

Hindmost Limited ('the company') was indebted to its bank ('Natland') on its overdraft to the extent of £100,000. Natland was worried about the fact that the loan was unsecured and in April 1986 insisted that the company execute a debenture in its favour, secured by a floating charge over the company's entire undertaking. The bank also insisted that the floating charge should contain clauses prohibiting the creation of any other charges or securities which would rank in priority to or pari passu with its floating charge, allowing it to crystallise the charge by the service of notice on the company, and providing that in the event of any enforcement proceedings being taken against the company, the floating charge would automatically crystallise on the first day of such proceedings.

Between April 1986 and January 1987, the company continued to trade, but experienced bigger and bigger losses. The overdraft rose to £150,000 and in breach of its undertaking the company borrowed £100,000 from Shark Finance plc and secured this by a charge over its factory. In February 1987, Jack, the company secretary, who was owed some £3,000 for salary which had not been paid for 2 months, instituted proceedings against the company. In March, Natland suspicious of what was happening, served a notice on the company crystallising the charge and later that month Jack served a winding-up petition on the company. A winding-up order was granted at the end of May.

Advise the liquidator, who has established that there is no more than £30,000 in the company, in what order to rank the claims by Natland, Shark Finance and Jack.

University of London LLB Examination
(for External Students) Company Law June 1987 Q7

General comment

The question is again of a fairly similar kind to the previous ones.

Skeleton solution

Liquidation is retrospective to the date of the petition. Definition of floating charge - concept of negative pledge clause - uncertain whether automatic crystallisation clauses are valid. A floating charge may be invalidated under IA s245.

Note J's locus standi to petition for winding up. Also possible fraudulent/wrongful trading under IA ss213, 214.

Suggested solution

The company entered liquidation in March, since it is the date of presentation of the petition which is the crucial date. This is important because of the provisions of the Insolvency Act (IA), discussed below, which allow for the setting aside of transactions entered into within a certain time before the commencement of the liquidation.

A debenture is a document evidencing the company's indebtedness, which is usually secured by a fixed and/or floating charge. Here a floating charge has been issued to Natland; this was defined by Romer LJ in *Re Yorkshire Woolcombers* (1903) as possessing the following three characteristics: first, it is a charge over assets present and future; second, those assets would in the ordinary course of business change; third, the charge continues to float unless and until some event causes it to crystallise; until that time the company is free to deal with the assets which are subject to the floating charge. This last point is a great practical advantage to the company, but it may be necessary for the creditor to act promptly if his security appears to be in danger. In an effort to gain extra protection the holders of floating charges began to insert in them restrictive clauses forbidding the company to create later charges which ranked in priority to the earlier ones. Such clauses are valid, but are construed strictly (*Robson v Smith* (1895)) but their effectiveness as against the holders of later fixed charges depends upon those holders having actual notice of the earlier charge and the restrictive clause. Registration under Companies Act s395 gives constructive notice of the former but not of the latter: *Wilson v Kelland* (1910).

Natland has a charge with a restrictive clause but Shark has probably obtained priority over the floating charge in view of the observations in the previous paragraph. In order to overcome this the Bank will have to argue that their charge had become fixed before the charge was granted to Shark. The success of this argument depends upon whether automatic crystallisation clauses are valid. It is settled that crystallisation happens on the appointment of a receiver or the commencement of a winding-up, and there is authority to suggest that the same happens where the business ceases to be a going concern: *Davey v Williamson* (1898); *Evans v Rival Granite* (1910); *Re Woodroffes (Musical Instruments) Ltd* (1986). However, there is no English authority to support an automatic crystallisation clause of the one encountered here. The policy objection to this solution, namely that a floating charge may become fixed without any current or later creditors being aware of the fact seems to have prevailed. The position is clearer in New Zealand where *Re Manurewa* (1971) is authority for the validity of automatic crystallisation clauses. This case is of no more than persuasive authority in this country, but it is interesting to note that in *Re Brightlife* (1986) Hoffmann J suggested that automatic crystallisation clauses might well be valid. The law in this area is in a state of flux at the present time.

If the charge is still a floating charge, then it is necessary to consider IA 1986 s245; the charge was granted within the twelve months prior to liquidation, but the Bank appears to have advanced cash after the charge was granted. It will thus be a secured creditor for £50,000, but unsecured for the rest.

Jack's locus standi to petition is not in doubt. IA 1986 ss122 and 123 give a creditor the right to petition for a winding up, and Jack satisfies the relevant definition.

There may also be questions of fraudulent or wrongful trading under IA ss213, 214;

these could lead to the imposition of personal liability on the directors of the company.

Jack's unpaid wages are a preferential debt in the liquidation. He ranks below the liquidator and the fixed charge, but above the floating charge. He is entitled to four months wages, up to a maximum of £800.

QUESTION 6

Jubilee Ltd was indebted to its sole director and majority shareholder, Ken, in the amount of £150,000. Ken knew that prospects for the company were bleak, but after discussing the matter with the manager of the Pity Bank, the following arrangement was arrived at. The bank agreed to make overdraft facilities of £150,000 available to the company in exchange for what was described as a 'first fixed charge' over the company's fixed assets and all book debts and other receivables, as well as a floating charge over the company's entire undertaking. The floating charge contained a restriction prohibiting the company from creating any other charges which might rank in priority to or equal with the floating charge. It also contained a clause, in terms of which the floating charge was to crystallize immediately on the initiation of any legal process against the company, or on any attempt by the company to create any prohibited charge.

These two charges were created in May 1987 and were duly registered. During the period June to December 1987, the company received some £200,000, but instead of holding this for the benefit of the bank, Ken used it to repay the company's indebtedness to himself, as well as to engage in further speculative ventures. The bank made no attempt to ensure that the money collected by the company was paid into a separate bank account over which it had control. Indeed, during this time the company also made use of the overdraft facilities to the extent of £100,000.

Early in December, the company borrowed £50,000 from the West Bank and deposited with that bank, as security for this loan, its title deeds to the factory which it owned. In mid-December, one of the company's employees, Larry, who had for the past 6 months, been paid only half his salary, presented a petition for the winding up of the company. There were protracted negotiations to stave off liquidation, but they failed and the winding up order was made in May 1988.

Apart from the factory, the company has movable assets worth no more than £10,000 and debts owing to it of some £40,000. The company's debts - including those mentioned above - are well in excess of £200,000.

Discuss.

University of London LLB Examination
(for External Students) Company Law June 1988 Q5

General comment

Like question 5, this one also features the possibility of wrongful trading. This originates from the Insolvency Act 1986, and it is to be expected that in future it will feature increasingly often in debenture questions.

Skeleton solution

Fixed charge registered under CA 1985 s395, but not as a land charge. Negative pledge clause binding only on those who know of both charge and restriction. Validity of automatic crystallisation is open to debate. Ken infringes IA s239 with loan to self, and may be guilty of wrongful trading. Note also IA s245 on floating charges created within one year of winding-up. Larry is a preferential creditor.

Suggested solution

The first fixed charge created by the company is registrable under Companies Act (CA) 1985 s395, and has been duly registered. However, in so far as in the charge relates to land it also requires to be registered under the Land Charges Act 1972. Failure to comply with this requirement will render the charge void against a subsequent purchaser for value of the legal estate.

A floating charge over the company's entire undertaking is registered at the same time. It contains a restriction prohibiting the company from creating any other charges ranking in priority to or equal with the floating charge. It is well established that subsequent chargees who would otherwise take free from the first charge will take free of the restriction unless they have notice of the charge and the restriction: *English and Scottish Mercantile Investment Co Ltd* v *Brunton* (1892). Registration of the charge does not give others constructive notice of the restriction: *Wilson* v *Kelland* (1910).

The validity of the automatic crystallisation clause is open to much debate. It is settled that crystallisation happens on the appointment of a receiver or the commencement of a winding-up, and there is authority to suggest that the same happens where the business ceases to be a going concern: *Davey* v *Williamson* (1898); *Evans* v *Rival Granite* (1910); *Re Woodroffes (Musical Instruments) Ltd* (1986). However, there is no English authority to support an automatic crystallisation clause of the type encountered here. The policy objection to this solution, namely that a floating charge may become fixed without any current or later creditors being aware of the fact seems to have prevailed for a long time. However, the decision of Hoffmann J in *Re Brightlife* (1986) does now lend some support to the idea that such clauses may be valid in this country. The position is more settled in New Zealand where *Re Manurewa* (1971) is clear authority for the validity of automatic crystallisation clauses.

In repaying the loan to himself Ken is clearly infringing Insolvency Act (IA) 1986 s239 by giving a preference to one creditor of the company (himself) ahead of other creditors. The preference will accordingly be void, and Ken may be required to repay the money to the company.

Ken may also be liable for wrongful trading under IA s214 in that he continued to trade knowing that the company could not meet its debts. It is less likely that actual dishonesty could be proved, which would be required for a charge of fraudulent trading under s213.

The borrowing of the £50,000 from the West Bank and the deposit of the factory's title deeds amount to an equitable charge on land,which is registrable under s395 and under the Land Charges Act (puisne mortgage - class C(i)).

Failure to register under the Companies Act makes the charge void and also renders the company and any officer in default liable to a fine.

Any floating charge created within one year of a winding-up may be invalid if the company was not solvent immediately after its creation, except to the extent that fresh consideration was provided: IA 1986 s245. Here an overdraft was granted, which appears to make the charge valid: *Re Yeovil Glove Co Ltd* (1965).

Larry is (as an employee) a preferential creditor in the liquidation for his salary for the four months preceding the commencement of the winding-up (here the date of the petition) up to a maximum of £800.

The order of payment is as follows:

1. Fixed Charge holders (Pity Bank)

2. Liquidators' expenses

3. Preferential creditors (Larry)

4. Crystallised floating charge holder (second charge)

5. Unregistered fixed charge (West Bank). If the charge is registered and the chargee has no actual notice of the restriction in the floating charge, the fixed charge will rank ahead of the floating charge.

9   CORPORATE RESCUE

9.1 Introduction

9.2 Key points

9.3 Recent cases and statutes

9.4 Analysis of questions

9.5 Question

9.1   Introduction

The concept of corporate rescue is a relatively modern one. Prior to the Insolvency Act of 1985 the emphasis when dealing with companies in financial difficulties was on winding up as a means of protecting creditors. The more modern notion is that greater efforts should be made to rescue the company so that it can continue in business.

9.2   Key points

a)   *Context*

The notion of corporate rescue arises in cases where companies are in some financial difficulty, but it is thought that there is still a reasonable prospect of saving them from total collapse. The introduction of the Administration Order regime reflects a change in attitude in the direction of saving companies wherever possible.

b)   *Obtaining an order*

Directors, creditors or the company may petition for an Administration Order. The Order will be made if it appears that the company is unable to pay its debts and the court is of opinion that the purpose of the Order, namely securing the continuance of the business as a going concern, can be achieved.

Alternatively an Order may be made for the purpose of enabling a voluntary composition with creditors or in order to effect a more advantageous realisation of the company's assets than could be achieved on a winding-up.

c)   *The effect of the order*

Once an Order has been made no winding-up petition may be presented (and any existing petition will be dismissed). No security may be enforced against the company without the leave of the court.

d)   *The administrator*

The Administrator must be a qualified Insolvency Practitioner. He is appointed by the Court and is at all times under the direction of the court.

The Administrator has extensive powers, including the removal of directors and the conduct of the company's business. He is the agent of the company.

The Administrator has three months from the date of his appointment in which to formulate proposals for ensuring the survival of the company. These proposals will be sent to the Registrar of Companies, and must also be laid before a meeting of the creditors. Before any scheme can be implemented it must be approved both by the creditors and by the Administrator.

One possible defect in the Administration Order regime is that chargees are still entitled to appoint their own receivers, and chargees will retain their existing place in the order of creditors. So far as the unsecured creditors are concerned this may well mean that the success of the new system will depend upon the co-operation and goodwill of those holding fixed or floating charges.

9.3   Recent cases and statutes

The Insolvency Act 1986 introduced into English law the concept of the Administration Order, which lies at the heart of the scheme of corporate rescue which is considered in this chapter.

9.4   Analysis of questions

The only appearance so far of this topic on the London LLB External examination is an essay question in 1987. For the moment it seems likely that essay questions will pre-dominate, not least since there is not enough case-law to allow a sensible discussion in problem form.

9.5   Question

'Radical recent changes will make a substantial difference to the regimes governing insolvent companies. Since the passage of the Insolvency Act, first in 1985, then in 1986, there is a real chance to save and rehabilitate insolvent companies.' Discuss.

University of London LLB Examination
(for External Students) Company Law June 1987 Q1(b)

General comment

This is likely to be fairly typical of the essay questions which will be set in this area. It invites a general review of the new system of Administration Orders, with some allusion to the previous law. As yet there is very little authority in this area, so it is necessary to concentrate on the statutory provisions. No doubt this balance will change in years to come.

Skeleton solution

New scheme forces earlier consideration of possible insolvency. Note also penalties for wrongful/fraudulent trading and possibility of disqualification order against directors.

New role of 'Administrator' whose job is to try to rescue the company. Application by company, director or creditor. Appointment stays other proceedings to wind-up or enforce security. Administrator makes proposals to creditors for rescuing company. Procedure is as yet untested, but success may depend on goodwill of chargees.

Suggested solution

The new Act will force directors to consider the financial position of the company far sooner than before and to put into operation new provisions which enable the company to seek rescue. This earlier examination of the company's position, while not necessarily avoiding insolvency, may bring about more satisfactory results for members and creditors alike. The Act imposes sanctions for wrongful and fraudulent trading, which are designed to ensure that directors do in fact look at the position at the proper time. The provisions of the Company Directors Disqualification Act should also encourage directors to be careful.

The Act provides for the appointment of an Administrator, an office not unknown in other jurisdictions. The other office through which a rescue may be effected is that of administrative receiver. This is similar to the old receiver/manager. He will take charge of all or substantially all the company's property, but he is under no duty to rescue the company; instead his main duty is to pay off the debt secured by the charge under which he was appointed, having first satisfied preferential creditors. Thus, the new development is that of the Administrator, and his role must be examined in more detail.

The administration procedure is designed as a vehicle through which ailing companies may be rescued - see eg s8(3), which provides that an administration order is made to secure the survival of the company as a going concern. The other possible purposes for an order would be the approving of a voluntary arrangement under Part I of the Insolvency Act (IA), the sanctioning of a compromise or arrangement under Companies Act (CA) s423 or a more advantageous realisation of the company's assets than would be effected on a winding-up.

The court will make the order if the company is unable to pay its debts (IA s123) and the court is satisfied that the purpose of the order can be achieved.

Directors, creditors or the company itself may apply for such an order - IA s9. Notice of the application must be given to anyone who is entitled to appoint an administrative receiver and the order will not be made where an administrative receiver is already in place unless the person who appointed him consents.

Once an order has been applied for no winding-up resolution can be passed and no security can be enforced against the company without the court's consent. The making of an order will ensure the dismissal of any outstanding winding-up petition and the vacation of office by any existing administrative receiver.

The Administrator, who must be a qualified Insolvency Practitioner, has considerable powers. He can manage the affairs, property and business of the company, he can deal with charged property, remove directors and require information from the officers and employees of the company. He will be the agent of the company. He has three months in which to formulate proposals, which must be sent to the Registrar of

Companies and laid before a meeting of the creditors. The latter will consider them and may suggest modifications, subject to the approval of the administrator.

Having been appointed by the court, the Administrator will at all times be under the direction of the court. This may prove to be one of the great strengths of the new procedure, since the administrator will be non-partisan, in contrast to the administrative receiver, who is necessarily acting on behalf of the person who appoints him. Perhaps the major disadvantage of the new procedure is the lapse of time between applying for an order and obtaining it. This will leave chargees time to insert their own receiver. Thus, it appears that the success of the scheme may well depend on the goodwill of chargees.

10   LIQUIDATIONS

10.1   Introduction

10.2   Key points

10.3   Recent cases and statutes

10.4   Analysis of questions

10.5   Questions

10.1   Introduction

This chapter deals with some of the problems which arise when a company goes into liquidation. As these problems can be spread over a wide spectrum of company law, there is a certain amount of cross-referencing.

10.2   Key points

a)   *Role of liquidator*

When a company goes into liquidation, whether voluntary or compulsory, it is the duty of the liquidator to collect in all debts due to the company and to settle, in so far as the assets permit, all debts owed by the company. Three major types of problem arise. The first is that of establishing which claims on the company are valid. Potential creditors may seek to assert claims which are of doubtful legal validity. The second type of problem arises mainly in insolvent liquidations. The liquidator must take care to pay claims in the order prescribed by statute. It is likely that some creditors will seek to have their claim classified in a higher category than that to which it properly belongs. The liquidator will have to deal with attempts of this kind. The third type of problem concerns the examination of the conduct of directors and other employees of the company. If there has been misconduct, then it may become the duty of the liquidator to take action against the individuals who are in default.

b)   *Validity of claims*

The major area of difficulty here arises in connection with retention of title clauses. These are clauses contained in contracts for the sale of goods which purport to reserve title in the goods to the seller until the goods are paid for in full. A more extreme variant of these clauses is found where the parties deal on the basis of a rolling account. In such cases the clause may provide that no title to any goods supplied is to pass unless the account is entirely clear. The effect of this can be to prevent the passage of title even to goods which have been fully paid for.

The validity in principle of retention of title clauses was accepted by the Court of Appeal in *Aluminium Industrien Vaassen BV* v *Romalpa Aluminium Ltd* [1976] 2 All ER 552. Subsequent cases have, however, severely restricted the ambit of the principle, holding that the right to reclaim the goods can be lost if they are irretrievably mixed with other goods, and that in any event the right created in favour of the seller may well amount to a charge on the goods such as requires to be registered under CA 1985 s395 and is void in the absence of such registration: *Borden (UK) Ltd v Scottish Timber* [1981] Ch 25, *Re Bond Worth Ltd* [1980] Ch 228, *Re Peachdart Ltd* [1984] Ch 131. At the present day it is fair to say that the courts look with disfavour on retention of title clauses, and will often find some way of rendering them ineffective if not actually void.

c) *Order of priority*

CA 1985 provides that the first charge in a liquidation is the costs and expenses of the liquidation, followed by satisfaction of the fixed charges, then preferential creditors (including employees up to four months wages or £800, the Inland Revenue and the Customs and Excise for one year's arrears). Next come the holders of floating charges, then the unsecured creditors. The final creditors are the deferred creditors, after which any surplus is distributed to the members.

Because of the above order of priorities it may be important to know whether a particular charge is valid. This may depend upon whether it has been duly registered at the Companies Registry under CA 1985 s395. There may also be questions about the date at which a charge crystallised, and an important area of dispute here concerns automatic crystallisation clauses, which are dealt with in chapter 8: *Debentures*.

d) *Misconduct*

As a general rule shareholders and officers of a company are not liable for the company's losses beyond, in the case of the shareholders, the paid-up amount of the share capital. This principle may not apply where there has been misconduct. The most blatant form of this arises where the company's funds have been fraudulently misappropriated. In such cases it may be necessary to consider criminal as well as civil proceedings. Misconduct may also take the form of wrongfully authorising payments to a director or to a person or company connected with a director, and here there may be civil proceedings for the recovery of the money. Finally, the questions of wrongful and/or fraudulent trading under IA 1986 ss213-214 may arise. Wrongful trading occurs where the directors carry on business knowing that the company is unable to meet its debts. Fraudulent trading means carrying on business for the purpose of defrauding creditors. It is a criminal offence and liability may be incurred by anyone who is party to it, not just by the directors of the company.

10.3   Recent cases and statutes

Insolvency Act 1986: revamped the law on the dissolution of companies. Introduced the new concepts of wrongful and fraudulent trading.

Re Andrabell Ltd [1984] 3 All ER 407, *Clough Mill Ltd* v *Martin* [1984] 3 All ER 982; these cases provide further consideration of the validity and effect of *Romalpa* clauses.

10.4   Analysis of questions

This is a topic which is closely connected with that of debentures, since it is for the most part only when a company goes into liquidation that questions about the validity and priority of debentures come to the fore. Students will appreciate that in view of this it is wise to prepare either both topics or neither. These aspects of liquidation have been considered at length in chapter 8: *Debentures* and will not be repeated here. There are, though, a number of other important points arising in connection with liquidations, and these are examined in this chapter.

10.5   Questions

Type 1:   Retention of title clauses

QUESTION 1

Nott Ltd supplied rubber to Plop Ltd under a retention of title clause which obliged Plop Ltd to keep the proceeds of sale of the rubber in a separate bank account. Plop Ltd made the rubber into tyres, which they then sold (under a retention of title clause) to Redd Ltd, who put the tyres on the cars which they made. Redd Ltd supplied the cars to their distributors, who sold a number of them to purchasers under conditional sale contracts, which provided that title to the car should not pass until payment had been made in full. Plop Ltd are now in insolvent liquidation, and Tim, who bought one of the cars from a dealer, has crashed it, damaging it beyond repair. At the time of the accident Tim had not finished paying for the car. Discuss.

Written by Editor
November 1989

General comment

This is a somewhat tricky problem involving multiple title retention clauses of different types.

Skeleton solution

Nott-Plop: clause valid, but no effective remedy for breach. Probably a charge over assets, so security void if not registered.

Plop-Redd: clause valid and tyres are removable from Redd's cars. Unlikely that Plop can assert title against any subsequent purchaser of the car.

Dealer-Tim: Dealer retains title, but Tim must still pay, presumably out of the insurance proceeds.

Suggested solution

Retention of title clauses are common in commercial sales. In principle they appear to be valid as between the parties, as was held in the *Romalpa* case (1976), but there are difficulties when third parties become involved. Where the purchaser is a company there is the further possibility that the clause will be held to create a charge on the company's assets, which is void under Companies Act 1985 s395 if not registered within twenty-one days of its creation. In the present case there are a number of sales, which need to be considered separately.

Nott-Plop sale

The obligation to keep the money in a separate account is probably valid, but it is hard to see what effective sanction can be applied if this is breached. A breach would presumably be a breach of contract or trust by the company, but the only remedy would be a damages action against the company; as it is in insolvent liquidation, there is presumably no money available to meet the claim anyway. If the clause is complied with, it may be possible to argue for the existence of a trust, but even this now seems uncertain. It seems likely that this is a case of a charge over assets - it will be impossible to trace the original rubber, since it will have become mixed into a finished product: *Borden (UK) Ltd* v *Scottish Timber* (1979); *Re Bond Worth* (1980). As there is no evidence of registration having taken place, it seems likely that Nott have no effective remedy available.

Plop-Redd sale

As between Plop and Redd this may be effective in practice as well as in theory, since the tyres are presumably severable from the cars, at least in so far as Redd still have them. To this extent it is, therefore, probably unnecessary to resort to the notion of a charge over assets. It is thought, though, that the lack of title to the tyres will not prevent Redd from giving their dealers good titles to cars supplied to them, so that Plop cannot reclaim vehicles in the hands of the dealers. What is less clear is whether Plop can seek to reclaim the tyres from those vehicles. Again, it is thought that they probably cannot, although the point is not directly covered by authority, it is clear that judicial attitudes are becoming more hostile to retention of title clauses, and it seems unlikely that the clause would be considered enforceable against a third party. In this situation it seems that Plop will again have no worthwhile remedy, since they apparently have no way of registering a charge over the assets of Redd, even assuming that they know what has become of their tyres.

Dealer-Tim sale

Presumably the car still belongs to the dealer, though Tim must have some interest in it. It is impracticable for the dealer to seek to reclaim the wreckage. At the same time the crash does not relieve Tim of the obligation to pay for the car, which he may well have to do out of the insurance proceeds, if any.

Thus, it seems likely that none of the retention of title clauses will be of much practical use in this case. This outcome reflects the general problems of these clauses, namely that many of them will be void if not registered and that even those which are in principle valid lose much of their usefulness once the goods pass into the hands of third parties or are incorporated into some other finished product.

Type 2: Conduct of liquidations

QUESTION 2

In May 1989 Pop Ltd agreed to buy Cherry's shares in Orange Ltd for £250,000. The following events then happened in the order listed.

Orange Ltd sold machinery parts, surplus to its requirements, to Pop Ltd for £40,000. Pop Ltd re-sold them for £60,000.

Pop Ltd borrowed £70,000 from a bank.

Cherry transferred her shares in Orange Ltd to Pop Ltd for £150,000 in cash; she also resigned as a director of Orange Ltd. At the same time she was paid by Orange Ltd £40,000 in 'compensation for loss of office' and was appointed a consultant to the company for two years at £30,000 per annum.

Orange Ltd paid £70,000 from its distributable profits to the bank in discharge of Pop Ltd's indebtedness.

Orange Ltd has just gone into insolvent liquidation. Advise the liquidator.

Written by Editor
October 1989

General comment

This is a very mixed question, containing a number of different points which are likely to concern the liquidator.

Skeleton solution

Sale of machinery may be misfeasance - £40,000 compensation recoverable from Cherry unless approved by company in General Meeting - consultancy fee proper only if Cherry actually works for the company - payment of £70,000 almost certainly improper - may be recovered from directors or payee.

Note generally IA ss213, 214 on fraudulent/wrongful trading.

Suggested solution

The question suggests that the machinery parts may have been sold at an undervalue of some £20,000. This could possibly amount to misfeasance by the directors of Orange Ltd, and is a matter which the liquidator ought to investigate. In the absence of a proper explanation, he should consider taking action against the directors. In this context Cherry's position is particularly open to question. One interpretation of the facts given would be that Cherry was seeking to benefit Pop Ltd in return for their agreement to buy her shares. It is also to be observed that Pop Ltd ultimately does not pay in full the agreed purchase price of the shares. Although this is not directly relevant to the liquidation, since it is a matter between Cherry and Pop Ltd, it may be seen as further evidence of wrongdoing by Cherry.

On resigning her directorship Cherry received £40,000 compensation. Companies Act 1985 s311 requires that details of such compensation be disclosed to the company and approved by it. It is unclear whether this was done in the present case. If not, it is suggested that the liquidator may be able to recover the money from Cherry.

As regards the appointment as consultant, this does not appear to be subject to the s319 requirement of approval by the general meeting, since it is not an appointment to a directorship. Nevertheless, the liquidator would do well to investigate the circumstances of the appointment, and in particular to check whether Cherry has in fact been working as a consultant.

The payment of the £70,000 in discharge of Pop Ltd's indebtedness also looks extremely suspicious. It is very hard to understand how the making of this payment can have been in the best interests of Orange Ltd, and the liquidator should certainly investigate the circumstances in which it came to be made. There is a distinct possibility that the directors of Orange Ltd can be made personally liable for this wrongful dissipation of the company's assets, or that the money can be recovered from Pop Ltd: *Aveling Barford Ltd* v *Perion Ltd* (1989).

A more general question which arises from any insolvent liquidation is whether the directors have carried on business knowing that the company was unable to meet its debts (in which case they can be made personally liable for wrongful trading - Insolvency Act (IA) 1986 s213) or whether they have sought to defraud any of the creditors by carrying on business knowing of the insolvency, in which case they may be criminally liable for fraudulent trading - IA 1986 s214.

In summary, the liquidator should be advised to investigate very carefully the circumstances of and justification for all these transactions. If not satisfied by the explanations which he receives, he should consider taking action against the directors of Orange Ltd (especially Cherry) and/or against Pop Ltd for recovery of sums wrongfully paid.

Type 3: Wrongful trading

Wrongful and fraudulent trading are new concepts originating in the Insolvency Act 1986. In any question involving the liquidation of a company it may be necessary to consider whether either of these offences has been committed. For an example of a question involving these matters see question 3 in chapter 12: *Directors*.

11   MEETINGS

11.1   Introduction

11.2   Key points

11.3   Recent cases and statutes

11.4   Analysis of questions

11.5   Questions

11.1   Introduction

This chapter examines problems which may arise in connection with the conduct of a company's general meeting. There is considerable overlap with, and cross-referencing to chapter 13, which deals with the treatment of minorities.

11.2   Key points

a)   *Calling of meetings*

Due notice of a company meeting must be given. This will be twenty-one days in the case of the AGM (Annual General Meeting), fourteen days in the case of an EGM (Extraordinary General Meeting) (unless a Special Resolution is proposed, in which case the notice reverts to twenty-one days). Notice must be given to all those entitled to attend and vote, and the notice must state the nature of the business with sufficient particularity to enable members to decide whether or not they wish to attend. Short notice may validly be accepted by all those entitled to attend and vote at an AGM or by holders of 95% of the votes in the case of an EGM.

Not more than fifteen months may elapse between one AGM and the next (CA 1985 s366).

Holders of 10% of the votes may require the board to call an EGM (s368) and the court has power to call a meeting if the directors at any time wrongfully fail to do so (s371).

b)   *Procedure at meetings*

The chairman is elected by the meeting (s370(5)). It is customary for the chairman of the board to chair the meeting, but there is no automatic right for him to do so.

When a vote is taken on any proposal a show of hands is initially taken. The result of this is binding unless a poll is validly demanded. The chairman is always entitled to insist on a poll, and a valid demand may also be made by the holders of at least 10% of the votes or by any five members of the company present in person. On a poll each shareholder has one vote per share, whereas on a show of hands each person present has one vote. On a poll proxy votes may also be taken into consideration.

An Ordinary Resolution requires only a simple majority of votes cast, whereas Special and Extraordinary Resolutions require 75% of the votes cast.

Where there is an equality of votes on a resolution the chairman has a second or casting vote.

Subject to any contrary provision in the articles the meeting is quorate so long as two members are present in person. This means that one member in person plus a proxy for a second member is not a quorum, nor is there a quorum if only one member attends, even if he holds proxies for several others. Although there is no express statutory provision as to the status of business purportedly transacted at an adjourned meeting, it is thought that such proceedings would be ineffective. To come to any other conclusion would vitiate the purpose of having quorum requirements: *Byng* v *London Life Association Ltd* [1989] 1 All ER 560.

The chairman may adjourn the meeting from time to time with the consent of those present. As a general rule he has no right unilaterally to adjourn. If he attempts to do so, it appears that the remaining members can properly continue the meeting without him, electing a new chairman for the purpose. An inquorate meeting may also validly be adjourned, since it is a meeting, notwithstanding that it cannot transact any business: *Byng* v *London Life Association Ltd* [1989] 1 All ER 560.

11.3   Recent cases and statutes

Byng v *London Life Association Ltd* [1989] 1 All ER 560: deals with the constitutional status of an inquorate meeting and the Chairman's power to adjourn such a meeting.

11.4   Analysis of questions

This is an area which tends to be unpopular with students, perhaps because the relevant rules are something of a minefield. Since 1983 it has arisen only twice on the London LLB External paper, but it is fairly popular elsewhere. The two questions concerned are 1984 Q4 and 1986 Q8, both of which are fully dealt with in chapter 13 (questions 3 and 2). Their inclusion in the chapter on minorities points to an important practical aspect of this area of the law, namely that complaints are most likely to be made by those who have lost at the meeting, and the basis of the complaints is most likely to be that they as a minority are being unfairly treated.

The topic is potentially a large one, and this chapter contains a number of questions which have not appeared on the London paper, but which serve to illustrate the range of possibilities.

11.5   Questions

QUESTION 1

Yonks Ltd has its AGM. A Special Resolution is proposed, which is backed by the chairman. On a show of hands there are 30 votes in favour and 18 against. The chairman then says 'I have here a number of proxies in respect of this resolution. Seventy members have cast proxy votes for the resolution, ten have voted against. I therefore declare the resolution carried'. Another (Ordinary) resolution is carried on a show of hands by 24 votes to 23. The chairman, who opposes the resolution, says 'the Articles give me a second vote on any resolution. I cast that vote against this resolution, so there is a tie, and I declare the motion lost.' Mary, a shareholder, demands a poll on the resolution, but the chairman refuses to allow this. Discuss.

Written by Editor
July 1989

General comment

This question requires careful attention to the rules on voting at general meetings.

Skeleton solution

SR: result depends on number of votes carried by the various shareholders, not on the number voting. Answer cannot be determined from information supplied.

OR: chairman has casting vote only when there is already a tie, so the OR was passed. Mary may demand a poll if she has 10 per cent of the shares or if support by four other shareholders.

Suggested solution

The first resolution is a Special Resolution (SR) and therefore requires to be supported by three-quarters of the votes cast in relation to it. It is therefore clear that on the show of hands the resolution is lost, since 30 is less than 75% of 48. However, the chairman of the meeting is always entitled to demand a poll. On a poll one vote is cast in respect of each share held, rather than one vote for each shareholder, as is the case on a show of hands. It is open to question here whether the chairman has validly called a poll - he has not stated that he is doing so. Nevertheless, it is submitted that his actions are only consistent with the calling of a poll, and it is therefore likely that he would be treated as having exercised his right to do this. The next question is whether the SR is passed on the poll. If we add up the number of shareholders who have voted on the show of hands and the poll there are 100 in favour and only 28 against, and it may therefore appear that the necessary majority has been obtained. However, this is not the proper way to count the votes. It is necessary to look at how many shares are held by each of the persons who have voted. Only if there is a 75% majority of voting shares in favour of the SR will it be passed on the poll. The question does not contain the information necessary to determine this.

With regard to the second resolution the chairman has not stated the position correctly. The articles give him a second and casting vote only in the event that there is a tie when the votes are first cast. This has not happened here, and the consequence is that the Ordinary Resolution (OR) is passed on the show of hands.

Mary then calls for a poll, but it is necessary to enquire whether she has the power to do this. To make a valid demand for a poll an individual shareholder must have at least 10% of the votes, and it is unclear whether Mary has this. Alternatively, any five shareholders may combine to demand a poll, so Mary's demand will be valid if she can get four others to support her. If the demand is valid, then the chairman has acted wrongfully in refusing it, and Mary may be able to get the OR declared invalid by the court if she acts quickly enough.

QUESTION 2

Outline the formalities required for the calling of a company general meeting. Are the existing requirements sufficient to protect the interests of all concerned?

General comment

For the most part this is a straightforward essay question, which merely requires a thorough knowledge of the relevant statutory provisions. The final part of the question does, however, call for some critical comment on the present rules, and it is no doubt on this part of the answer that the good student's ability will become apparent.

Written by Editor
July 1989

Skeleton solution

Distinguish AGMs and EGMs: AGM each year - 21 days notice required, unless short notice procedure followed.

EGM when called by directors or requisitioned by 10 per cent of members. 14 days notice needed.

Notice of meeting must specify business to be transacted.

Rules provide reasonable balance between too many GMs and too few, though creditors are entirely unprotected.

Suggested solution

Company general meetings fall into two types, the Annual General Meeting (AGM) and Extraordinary General Meetings (EGMs). All meetings other than the AGM are EGMs.

An AGM must be held at least once in every calendar year, and no more than 15 months may elapse between AGMs. However, so long as a company holds its first AGM within 18 months of incorporation, it need not hold an AGM in the year of incorporation or in the following year (s366). Twenty-one days' notice is required for the AGM, unless the articles provide for a longer period. Short notice is acceptable if consented to by all the members entitled to attend and vote at the AGM (s369(3)). The method of giving notice is specified in the articles, but will normally be by post to all members.

Holders of 10% of the votes may require the board to call an EGM (s368) and the court has power to call a meeting if the directors at any time wrongfully fail to do so (s371).

The notice of the meeting must specify the business to be transacted with sufficient particularity to enable members to decide whether or not to attend.

EGMs by definition do not happen at regular intervals. Normally the calling of them is at the discretion of the board, but attention is drawn to s368 (mentioned above). Only 14 days notice is required for an EGM.

The question also asks about the protection of relevant interests. This is a difficult issue, since it is not clear that the rules really aim to protect any particular interest. As usual in company law it is possible to identify the shareholders, the directors and the creditors as three groups whose interests must be balanced. The GM is the residual authority within the company, retaining any powers which have not been delegated to the directors. From the directors' point of view it is important not to have too many GMs, since they are liable to interfere with the smooth running of the company. This may explain the rule that the calling of EGMs is normally to be left to the directors. At the same time it is necessary to have some GMs, so that the shareholders can be kept informed and can have the chance to express their views on important matters of company policy. Thus, there must be at least one GM in each year. The s368 power to requisition a meeting is also relevant in this context, since it provides a way in which a disaffected minority can air some of their grievances. In terms of controlling the directors the requirement of giving details of the business may also be mentioned. This operates to prevent unannounced resolutions from being slipped through a GM.

In general, therefore, the conclusion seems to be that the rules provide a reasonable balance between the directors and the shareholders. It is to be observed, though, that the interests of the creditors do not seem to be treated as being of any relevance here. Admittedly, it is hard to see what can be done about this, particularly since creditors have no right to attend the meeting anyway.

QUESTION 3

Nemo Ltd has its AGM. Achilles, a shareholder having 11% of the shares, attends. The articles of Nemo Ltd state that the quorum for a general meeting is ten. Only eight people turn up, but the chairman announces his intention to proceed with the meeting nevertheless. An ordinary resolution is proposed, which Achilles opposes. The chairman declares the motion carried on a show of hands. Achilles demands a poll, but the chairman ignores him and declares the meeting adjourned until the following week. At the adjourned meeting, which Achilles does not attend, but which is clearly quorate, a Special Resolution is passed, altering the articles of association so as to prevent any shareholder from demanding a poll at general meetings of the company. In addition, an Ordinary Resolution is passed declaring valid the events at the meeting the week before. Advise Achilles.

Written by Editor
October 1989

General comment

This is another question aimed at certain procedural aspects of general meetings.

Skeleton solution

Meeting is inquorate. A is probably entitled to have proceedings declared invalid.

A was entitled to a poll, but the result would probably have been the same. Passage of SR at adjourned meeting is probably invalid.

Suggested solution

The first point is that the meeting is inquorate. Table A articles do not expressly state what happens when business is purportedly transacted at an inquorate meeting, but it is generally understood that such proceedings are ineffective. Indeed, any other conclusion would entirely defeat the point of having quorum requirements. It therefore appears that the simplest solution for Achilles is to seek to have the proceedings at the first meeting declared invalid.

An alternative line of argument for Achilles would be that his demand for a poll was wrongfully ignored. As the holder of more than 10% of the voting shares Achilles is always entitled to require a poll. This too is potentially a ground for the negation of this resolution, though it must be pointed out that the court might be reluctant to grant any declaration if it appears that the resolution would have been passed even on the poll.

The question of the adjourned meeting is trickier. If the original meeting is inquorate, then the correct step is to adjourn it and make another attempt later. However, two difficulties arise about the events at the second meeting. The first is that it is unclear whether the Special Resolution (SR) was included in the agenda for the original meeting. If it was not, then it cannot be added at a later stage, since 21 days' notice is required for such a resolution, and only a week has passed since the original meeting. In any event, SRs cannot be added to the agenda of a meeting after it has been sent out to the members. If the proposal was on the original agenda, then the SR may be valid, though Achilles may have some claim to relief under Companies Act 1985 s459 if it appears that the passage of the resolution was aimed at him personally.

It is thought that the attempt retrospectively to validate what went on at the first meeting is ineffective. In so far as the events of the first meeting constituted a wrong against Achilles personally, he has a right of action against the company (and perhaps against the chairman) and it is well settled that such a right of action cannot be taken away by a resolution of the General Meeting.

12   DIRECTORS

12.1   Introduction

12.2   Key points

12.3   Recent cases and statutes

12.4   Analysis of questions

12.5   Questions

12.1   Introduction

This is a very large topic which has many different aspects to it. The major ones which students need to consider are fiduciary duties, removal of directors, insider dealing, loans to directors, fraud on the minority. These can come up in virtually any combination.

12.2   Key points

a)   *Fiduciary duties*

Directors owe a fiduciary duty to the company. They must always act bona fide in the best interests of the company. This test is partially subjective (good faith) and partly objective (in the best interests).

The duty is not owed to the shareholders (*Percival* v *Wright* [1902] 2 Ch 421) who are therefore not generally entitled to sue for damages for a breach of the duty, though the shareholders acting in the name of the company can bring such an action and may always remove a director.

There may be duties owed to shareholders in particular situations, such as where a takeover bid has been made: *Gething* v *Kilner* [1972] 1 WLR 337.

In small companies (sometimes called quasi-partnerships) where the directors and shareholders are the same persons, it has sometimes been held that the affairs of the company must be conducted in a way which recognises the equitable obligations existing among the participators. It is unclear whether the duties are owed as directors or as shareholders or both, but it is clear that these principles can place restrictions on the freedom of action of the directors.

CA 1985 s309 also requires the directors to have regard to the interests of the company's employees in general.

There appears to be no general duty to consider the interests of creditors. It is to be noted however, that the concepts of wrongful trading and fraudulent trading, which can operate to make directors personally liable, will in practice compel directors to have at least some regard to the interests of creditors.

Directors are expected to perform their duties with reasonable care and skill, but this appears to be a subjective test in that the court asks what could reasonably be expected of a person having the knowledge and skill of this director: *Re City Equitable Fire Insurance Co Ltd* [1925] Ch 407.

This idea, which derives mainly from the nineteenth century, is to some extent subverted by the prospects of personal liability and or disqualification under the modern legislation.

Directors are forbidden to make a secret profit from their dealings with the company, and may be required to account for any such profit. This extends to the notion that they must not take advantage of any commercial opportunity which comes their way in the performance of their duties as directors of the company, but must use it for the company's benefit (the so-called 'corporate opportunity doctrine').

b) *Removal of directors*

A director may always be removed by an Ordinary Resolution of the general meeting - CA 1985 s303.

In small private companies it is common to give a director enhanced voting rights on a resolution to remove him from office. The enhancement will normally be sufficient to make him effectively irremovable. Although such clauses appear to contravene the spirit of the legislation they were approved as valid by the House of Lords in *Bushell v Faith* [1970] AC 1099.

c) *Fraud on the minority*

One of the exceptions to the rule that the shareholders cannot bring an action against the directors for breach of duty arises where there has been a fraud on the minority, ie the affairs of the company are being conducted in a way which benefits the majority (including the directors) but deprives the minority of their legal rights. For more detail on this see section 13.2.

d) *Insider dealing*

Insider dealing occurs where a person connected with a company deals in the shares of that company on the basis of unpublished price sensitive information which he has and which he could reasonably have been expected to keep confidential. It is a criminal offence under the Company Securities (Insider Dealing) Act 1985.

To date there have been very few prosecutions under this Act, and it appears that the offence is difficult to detect and very difficult to prove.

It is a matter of some dispute whether insider dealing ought really to be a criminal offence. According to one view it is a distortion of the principles of a fair and free market, but the alternative view is that success in the market always depends upon information, and the possession of it should not be penalised.

12.3   Recent cases and statutes

The Insolvency Act 1986 created the new concepts of wrongful and fraudulent trading, which serve to extend the situations in which directors can be held personally liable for losses suffered by their companies.

The Company Directors Disqualification Act 1986 extends the circumstances in which directors can be disqualified from acting in that capacity in consequence of proved wrongdoing on their part in connection with company management.

12.4   Analysis of questions

The topic of directors is one of considerable importance in company law, and can reliably be expected to occur frequently on examination papers. With the exception of 1985 (which is generally regarded as having been a rather unbalanced paper) this area has occurred on the London LLB External every year since 1983. However, the very importance of the topic means that it can easily be combined with other areas of law, especially minority protection and liquidation. This chapter consequently contains a good deal of cross-referencing.

The topic of loans to directors has arisen only once on the London LLB External paper since 1983 and then in conjunction with insider trading. The question (1987 Q8) is fully covered in chapter 16 (question 1), to which reference should be made for a summary of the relevant rules. It is thought unlikely that this topic would make up an entire question by itself.

12.5   Questions

It is impossible to divide the questions in this area into types. Virtually any of the topics identified can arise in any combination, and, as appears below, other matters not dealt with in this chapter are also sometimes encountered.

For examples of problems about removal of directors which are really concerned with minority protection, see questions 2 and 3 in chapter 13. Other questions about the misuse of directors' powers in a small company are questions 1 and 4, also included in chapter 13. A question which is more centrally concerned with the process for removing a director is question 2 below.

QUESTION 1

Michael is the managing director and chairman of Construction plc, a civil engineering company. He learns that Product Ltd is about to put out to tender a contract for the construction of a new factory and arranges a meeting with Charles, the Chairman of Product Ltd. Charles promises Michael that Construction plc will be awarded the contract if Michael can arrange for the repayment of a debt of £50,000 owed by Charles. Cheques drawn on Construction plc's bank account require the signature of Michael and one other director. Michael persuades Neil, one of the other directors of Construction plc, to sign a blank cheque which Michael subsequently completes in favour of Charles' creditor. Neil agrees to Michael's request because

Michael arranges for Construction plc to make an interest-free loan to Neil to enable him to pay gambling debts.

Neil realises that when the news of the contract between Construction plc and Product Ltd is made public, the value of Construction plc's listed shares will rise. Using the loan made to him he purchases shares in Construction plc which he subsequently sells at a handsome profit. Within a few months Product Ltd's business collapses and it is wound up insolvent. The contract with Construction plc is worthless and there is little chance of Construction plc being paid in respect of the work it has done.

Advise Archie, a minority shareholder in Construction plc, who has just discovered these facts.

University of London LLB Examination
(for External Students) Company Law June 1983 Q5

General comment

This question, which is referred to in chapters 13 and 16, covers fiduciary duties, loans to directors, insider trading and *Foss* v *Harbottle* (1843). So extensive a question gives a student serious problems in organising the answer in a sensible way.

Skeleton solution

Director's duties owed to company only. Archie may bring derivative action (fraud on minority) but the law is vague as to when this will be permitted. Alternatively he may use CA 1985 s459. This is also a vague provision, but courts have taken a liberal attitude and this is probably best option.

Archie could also report the insider trading to the authorities.

Suggested solution

A director owes his fiduciary duties to the company alone; in particular he owes no such duty to the shareholders: *Percival* v *Wright* (1902). However, this general principle has been somewhat modified by subsequent authority. Thus, where the shares are held by only a few people, as in *Coleman* v *Myers* (1977), or where there is a special situation such as a takeover (*Briess* v *Woolley* (1954)), it is possible that in the modern law the director may be held to owe some limited duty of care to the shareholder. It is submitted, however, that the content of this duty must not be such as to create a conflict with the director's fiduciary duties to the company. Subject to these limited exceptions a shareholder cannot as such complain of a director's breaches of duty since the duties are not owed to him.

Archie will naturally be concerned about the repayment of the debt and the signature of Neil, which was influenced by an interest-free loan. It may be argued that Michael is in breach of his duty to the company in authorising repayment of the debt, though Michael could argue that Construction plc would not have obtained the contract but for this repayment. Archie has two possible causes of action. The first is a derivative action on the basis that there has been a fraud on the minority in the form of a breach of the director's duty of good faith. The derivative action is one in which the shareholder brings an action which derives from the company's right of action against the wrongdoer, the company being unwilling to take the action because the wrongdoer is in control of the company. It is necessary to show that there has been some fraud; mere negligence on the part of a director does not amount to fraud for these purposes (*Pavlides* v *Jensen* (1956)), but misappropriation of the company's property clearly does: *Cook* v *Deeks* (1916). The difficult cases are those where the directors are not fraudulent in the strict sense but are so negligent that they benefit themselves as well as causing a loss to the company (*Daniels* v *Daniels* (1978)), treated as cases of equitable fraud, a broader notion than fraud at common law. Problems are also caused by cases involving misappropriation of the 'money, property or advantages' of the company, such as *Burland* v *Earle* (1902). In some cases minority action is permitted, but in others it is not.

In the present case a director who arranges that his company shall pay the private debt of another individual is almost certainly in breach of his duty of good faith to the company; there can be no doubt at all that Neill is in breach of duty in signing a company cheque for personal gain. In order to bring an action Archie will need to show that the company has not brought any action because the wrongdoers are in control. In *Prudential Assurance Co Ltd* v *Newman Industries Ltd* (1980) Vinelott J gave a liberal interpretation to control, and held that there was no need to go through the formality of calling an EGM where it could be shown that the wrongdoers would inevitably be able to control the vote. The locus standi for a derivative action is determined as a preliminary issue (*Prudential Assurance* and *Estmanco* v *GLC* (1982)), so Archie will need to show at least a prima facie case of fraud. It is likely that he has enough evidence to do so in the present case, but this is not his only option. In the alternative he could petition for relief under Companies Act (CA) 1985 s459; an advantage of this mode of proceeding is that he can introduce other matters, such as the loan and Neill's insider trading, which would not be relevant to the derivative action. He need only show 'unfair prejudice' to himself in the way the company's affairs are being conducted. This is a vague test, but s459 does appear to be more liberal than CA s210, which it replaced, and Archie should have a reasonable chance of success. It may also be noted that the s75 petition presents no problems of locus standi, and that on such a petition the court can in any event order that the petitioner be allowed to bring an action in the name of the company.

A further point is that the interest-free loan cannot really be in the interests of the company and may well be in breach of CA 1985 s330, which imposes both civil and criminal liability.

Archie may also be inclined to warn the regulatory authorities about the insider trading. Insider trading is a criminal offence under the Company Securities (Insider Dealing) Act 1985, though the relatively few prosecutions in this area have shown that there are considerable difficulties of both definition and proof.

On balance, therefore, the best advice to Archie is to launch a s459 petition.

QUESTION 2

Freedom Publishers Ltd ('the company') is a private limited company with articles in the Form of Table A, with the addition of the following clause:

'In the event of there being a resolution before a general meeting to dismiss a director, that director's shares shall carry 3 times the normal number of votes.'

The company has issued 10,000 shares, which are held as to 2,000 each by the three directors, Karl, Fred and Rosa. The remaining 4,000 are distributed amongst ten or so shareholders. Karl and Fred have become disturbed by the fact that recently Rosa has taken up with a new boyfriend who is a member of a Fascist political party and they feel that Rosa might not be able to continue to support the progressive publishing policies of the company. They consult you to consider whether Rosa might be dismissed as a director, telling you that they are likely to be able to command the support of all the other shareholders (apart, obviously, from Rosa).

Advise Karl and Fred as to what course or courses of action they should follow.

University of London LLB Examination
(for External Students) Company Law June 1987 Q6

General comment

This apparently formidable question in fact provides an excellent opportunity for a student who is familiar with the procedures for removing directors, since it asks for a display of exactly that knowledge in the context of the particular facts presented. Mention of other matters, such as changes to the articles (chapter 4) and the rules relating to share issues (chapter 7) is also required. The question as originally set contains a particular oddity, in that the weighted voting clause is apparently insufficient to prevent the removal of a director. Confronted with what looks suspiciously like a mistake on the part of the examiner, students would be well advised to deal also with the situation which would arise if the weighted voting clause were effective.

Skeleton solution

Weighted voting clauses are permitted, but this one seems ineffective on arithmetical grounds.

If it were effective, the majority might seek to change the articles, but R could challenge this as not being bona fide. Excluding R from board meetings would be improper. On issue of further shares, consider authority to allot and pre-emption provisions.

Suggested solution

Companies Act (CA) 1985 s303 allows a company to remove a director from its board by means of an ordinary resolution of the company in general meeting, and at first sight this may seem the obvious course of action. However, the articles contain a weighted voting clause, such as was approved by the House of Lords in *Bushell* v *Faith* (1970). Such clauses appear to contravene the principle that a director is always removable by Ordinary Resolution, but in *Bushell* v *Faith* (1970) the House of Lords said that the clause merely affected the way in which the votes were counted on such a resolution, and therefore the likelihood of its being passed - this did not infringe the rule that such a resolution would be effective if passed. This is at best a tenuous distinction, but the decision is still regarded as good law. Although *Bushell* v *Faith* was a case of a quasi-partnership, the principle does not appear to be limited to such companies.

However, some attention to arithmetic may resolve the problem. There are 10,000 issued shares, of which Rosa holds 2,000. Fred and Karl expect to be able to obtain the support of all the other shareholders, which will be a total of 8,000. This will outvote Rosa's 6,000 (2,000 x 3). It therefore appears that a s303 resolution will succeed.

As an alternative to the solution presented above, it is worth considering what the position would be if the *Bushell* v *Faith* clause allowed, say, quintuple votes, so that Rosa could defeat the s303 resolution by 10,000 votes to 8,000. One possible approach would be to seek to remove the *Bushell* v *Faith* clause. CA 1985 s9 allows a company to alter its articles by special resolution and Karl and Fred could command the necessary majority. Rosa, as a shareholder, will presumably challenge the alteration as not being made bona fide in the best interests of the company. It has been suggested (*Greenhalgh* v *Arderne Cinemas* (1946)) that such an alteration must be for the benefit of the hypothetical individual member (a very difficult test to apply, since no such person exists) or that the alteration must not discriminate between the majority of shareholders and the disaffected minority. In *Clemens* v *Clemens* (1976) the former test was modified to ask whether the change benefitted the aggrieved member. This may, however, be too generous to the minority, since it would effectively give them a veto over any change in the articles. Nevertheless, *Clemens* v *Clemens* does show the need, at least in a small company, for the majority to have due regard to the interests of the minority. Here it would be necessary to show that it is in the company's interests to be able to remove 'rogue' directors. On the face of it this is a convincing argument, but the difficulty is that the company was set up on the basis that directors would be protected from removal. The point is thought to be a finely balanced one, and Fred and Karl are by no means certain to succeed.

An alternative strategy for Fred and Karl would be to exclude Rosa from Board Meetings. However, this is improper (*Pulbrook* v *Richmond Consolidated Mining Co* (1878)) - and Rosa could restrain such conduct by injunction.

The last possibility is an issue of further shares so as to reduce Rosa's holding to a level where the *Bushell* v *Faith* clause would no longer protect her. Section 80 authority for such an allotment is needed. If the articles do not already provide this, an Ordinary Resolution must be passed. Even then ss89-96 must be considered. These provide pre-emption rights for existing shareholders on an allotment of new shares for cash. If Rosa is able to exercise her pre-emption rights this will defeat any scheme to dilute her shareholding. Karl and Fred may try allotting for non-cash consideration, or may choose to ignore the pre-emption rights. The effect of the latter course is unclear. Section 92 would give Rosa the right to compensation for any loss, damage or expenses resulting from the breach (which might perhaps include the loss of her directorship) but it is thought that the validity of the allotment probably cannot be challenged. A more serious difficulty is that Rosa may challenge the allotment as having been made for an improper purpose. *Hogg* v *Cramphorn* (1967) and *Howard Smith* v *Ampol* (1973) show that in such cases the court is likely to refer the matter to a general meeting to decide whether the shares (which cannot be voted at the meeting in question) have been properly allotted. It appears from the statement of facts that Karl and Fred will command a majority at this meeting, so the allotment will be ratified. Rosa's only remaining hope would then be to argue that the issue was a fraud on the minority or a disregard of the equitable obligations upon which the company was founded, which would raise the issues discussed above in connection with changes to the articles of association.

QUESTION 3

Jubilee Ltd was indebted to its sole director and majority shareholder, Ken, in the amount of £150,000. Ken knew that prospects for the company were bleak, but after discussing the matter with the manager of the Pity Bank, the following arrangement was arrived at. The bank agreed to make overdraft facilities of £150,000 available to the company in exchange for what was described as a 'first fixed charge' over the company's fixed assets and all book debts and other receivables, as well as a floating charge over the company's entire undertaking. The floating charge contained a restriction prohibiting the company from creating any other charges which might rank in priority to or equal with the floating charge. It also contained a clause, in terms of which the floating charge was to crystallize immediately on the initiation of any legal process against the company, or on any attempt by the company to create any prohibited charge.

These two charges were created in May 1987 and were duly registered. During the period June to December 1987, the company received some £200,000, but instead of holding this for the benefit of the bank, Ken used it to repay the company's indebtedness to himself, as well as to engage in further speculative ventures. The bank made no attempt to ensure that the money collected by the company was paid into a separate bank account over which it had control. Indeed, during this time the company also made use of the overdraft facilities to the extent of £100,000.

Early in December, the company borrowed £50,000 from the West Bank and deposited with that bank, as security for this loan, its title deeds to the factory which it owned. In mid-December, one of the company's employees, Larry, who had for the past 6 months been paid only half his salary, presented a petition for the winding up of the company. There were protracted negotiations to stave off liquidation, but they failed and the winding up order was made in May 1988.

Apart from the factory, the company has movable assets worth no more than £10,000 and debts owing to it of some £40,000. The company's debts - including those mentioned above - are well in excess of £200,000.

Discuss.

University of London LLB Examination
(for External Students) Company Law June 1988 Q5

General comment

Another popular area of directors' duties is that relating to the possibility that a director will be held liable for fraudulent or wrongful trading in the event that the company goes into liquidation. The law in this area was radically altered by IA 1985 (now IA 1986) and the subject arose on the London LLB External paper for the first time in 1988.

This question is mostly concerned with the issues about crystallisation of charges and order of payment of creditors. For this aspect of the problem see question 6 in chapter 8: *Debentures*, where these issues are dealt with. As far as fraudulent and wrongful trading are concerned the following answer is suggested.

This answer serves to illustrate the points which are most likely to arise in this context, namely the making of a void preference, and the possibility of actions under ss213 and 214. Students should be careful to deal with all these possibilities, even if only to dismiss them on the particular facts.

Skeleton solution

Note preference under IA s239 and fraudulent/wrongful trading under IA ss213, 214.

Suggested solution

In repaying the loan to himself Ken is clearly infringing Insolvency Act (IA) 1986 s239 in that he is giving a preference to one creditor (himself) at the expense of the other creditors. The preference is void, and the liquidator can reclaim the money from Ken.

In addition, Ken may also be liable for wrongful trading under IA 1986 s214 for continuing to trade when he ought to have known that the company could not pay its debts. Fraudulent trading under s213 is also a possibility, though this is difficult to establish since it must be shown that Ken was actually dishonest.

13   MINORITIES

13.1   Introduction

13.2   Key points

13.3   Recent cases and statutes

13.4   Analysis of questions

13.5   Questions

13.1   Introduction

This chapter examines the various ways in which disaffected minority shareholders in a company can seek to restrain conduct by the majority which they regard as unfair and/or oppressive.

13.2   Key points

a)   *Majority rule*

The basic principle of company law is that decisions, both of the board of directors and of the general meeting, are taken by majority vote. Consequently, a person who loses the vote must accept this fact.

However, this principle is subject to exceptions. So far as the board of directors is concerned, it must be remembered that decisions are to be taken bona fide and in the best interests of the company, rather than for the personal benefit of the directors (for a fuller account of the position of directors see chapter 12). However, the directors' duties are generally owed to the company rather than to individual shareholders, so that a breach of duty will not normally give rise to an action by an aggrieved shareholder.

In the case of the general meeting the principle may be stated as being that the shareholders are entitled to vote according to their own personal interests. They owe no duty, either to the company or to the other shareholders, to vote according to any notion of fairness. However, there may be an exception to this principle in the case of small companies operating on the basis of mutual trust among the shareholders (such companies are commonly referred to as quasi-partnerships.) In such companies there may be a continuing obligation to treat other members in an equitable way according to the understanding upon which the company was set up: *Ebrahimi* v *Westbourne Galleries* [1973] AC 360; *Clemens* v *Clemens* [1976] 2 All ER 268.

b)   *Companies Act 1985 s459*

This section confers a more general protection on minority shareholders than is mentioned above. It gives the court discretion to relieve against any course of conduct in the running of the affairs of a company which is unfairly prejudicial to the interests of some part of the membership including at least the petitioning shareholder. This section replaces CA 1948 s210, which aimed to perform a similar role, but was widely regarded as unsatisfactory because of the very narrow interpretation which had been placed upon it by the courts. The new provision has been more generously treated, and orders have been made for the discontinuance of an oppressive course of conduct and for the buying out of the minority's shares by the majority. It is still not the case, though, that the minority can always get relief - it is up to the court to decide first whether the conduct is in truth unfairly prejudicial to the interests of the petitioner as a member of the company.

c) *Winding-up petitions*

A more drastic remedy which may be available to an aggrieved member is to petition for the winding-up of the company. Under Insolvency Act 1986 s122 the court has a general discretion to make such an order if it thinks it just and equitable to do so. The usual basis for petitions of this kind has been the breach of the equitable obligations arising in quasi-partnerships, as discussed above. In other cases it has been held that the company should be wound up because the substrastum of it has failed: *Re German Date Coffee Co Ltd* (1882) 20 Ch D 169.This is obviously a drastic remedy. It will not lightly be granted, and indeed an aggrieved shareholder should consider carefully before he seeks it. If the company is profitable, then winding-up is unlikely to be the most appropriate solution to the problem. It may be that this remedy is used less now than it used to be, because of the greater availability of lesser remedies under CA 1985 s459.

d) *Other remedies*

In appropriate circumstances the DTI may be asked to investigate the affairs of the company under CA 1985 Part XVII (as to this see further chapter 14), but this remedy is unlikely to be of much assistance to the aggrieved individual shareholder.

Where a decision of the directors or of the general meeting is so improper as to amount to a fraud on the minority shareholders it may be possible for the minority to bring a derivative action in the name of the company against the wrongdoers under one of the exceptions to the rule in *Foss* v *Harbottle* (1843) 2 Hare 461. However the ambit of this rule is limited, for most wrongs done to a company may be ratified by a resolution of the company in general meeting.

13.3   Recent cases and statutes

Smith v *Croft (No 2)* [1987] 3 All ER 909: in considering whether to allow the bringing of a minority action the court will have regard to the views of the independent shareholders (ie those other than the alleged wrongdoers) generally.

13.4   Analysis of questions

Minority protection is a topic of immense importance in company law, and it is not surprising that it occurs so frequently in examinations. On the London LLB External it has appeared every year since 1985, sometimes in more than one question on the same paper. It is also a topic which can very readily be combined with other areas of the syllabus, notably directors, rules as to shares and the Articles of Association. It is thus a topic which cannot safely be neglected by students - a student who is not familiar with the rules as to minority protection is in danger of being unable to attempt a problem question despite having prepared adequately all the other topics which it covers. This point is well illustrated by the first question included in this chapter. At the present time there do not appear to be major changes taking place in this area of the law - the most important change occurred in 1980 with the repeal and replacement of CA 1948 s210. There is still a certain tendency for examiners to ask about the value of this change, but otherwise the statute law in this area looks reasonably settled, though there is of course a growing body of case law, especially on CA 1985 s459, and it is important to be familiar with this.

13.5   Questions

QUESTION 1

James was a director and holder of 1/3 of the issued share capital of Omega Ltd. The relevant provisions of the articles of association were as follows:

'a)   Each director of the company shall receive £5,000 per annum and shall be entitled to receive not less than 6 months' notice of the intention of the company to remove him or her from office.

b)   Any shareholder desirous of transferring his shares shall first inform the directors, who may purchase the same at a fair value, but notwithstanding anything to the contrary, no transfer of shares shall take place without the approval of the directors of the company.'

James had not received any remuneration for two years and when he complained to Ken and Len (the other directors and the holders of the other 2/3 of the issued shares of the company) he was told to 'belt up'. Relations between James on the one hand and Ken and Len on the other deteriorated and when James tried to negotiate with Ken and Len to sell his shares, they offered him £1.50 per share, about 1/4 of the true value. When James refused, Ken and Len told him that they would never approve a transfer of his (James') shares to anyone else. James has now received notice of a forthcoming shareholders' meeting, with a motion on the agenda that he be dismissed as a director.

Discuss.

University of London LLB Examination
(for External Students) Company Law June 1983 Q8

General comment

This question is a complex one because it encompasses directors' service contracts, the s14 contract, rules as to transfer of shares and minority protection under CA 1985 s459 and IA 1986 s122. The minority protection point logically comes last in the answer, and cannot properly be attempted except in the light of the answers given to the earlier points. The following answer deals with the various difficulties.

Skeleton solution

J's contract is valid and in the articles. J probably has a right to enforce this provision of the articles.

J may petition under CA s459 for his shares to be bought out at a proper value.

J may also petition for winding-up under IA s122, but he may not want so drastic a remedy.

Suggested solution

First, it appears that James's service contract does not fall foul of Companies Act (CA) 1985 s319, since there is a notice provision which allows it to be terminated before the expiry of five years and is not limited to specified circumstances. James can be dismissed at six months notice, so his damages for wrongful dismissal would be limited to six months' salary, though his damages for unfair dismissal, if proved, could exceed this.

The service contract is also embodied in the articles. Under CA 1985 s14 the articles are a contract between each member and the company, and between member and member (*Hickman* v *Kent & Romney Marsh Sheepbreeders' Association* (1915), *Rayfield* v *Hands* (1960)) but this contract protects only the members rights as a member, not his rights in any other capacity, such as solicitor (*Eley* v *Positive Government Life Assurance* (1876), promoter (*Melhado* v *Porto Alegre Railway Co* (1874)) or director (*Beattie* v *Beattie* (1938)). In this case the directors are ignoring not only the notice provision but also the transfer provision because they are not offering a fair value. The question is whether James can enforce the observance of the articles; in *Salmon* v *Quin & Axtens* (1909) two managing directors had a right of veto over each other's actions on a number of matters (this right was enshrined in the articles). One managing director ignored this right of veto and forced through in General Meeting a resolution authorising him to act. The other managing director brought a successful action on behalf of himself and all other wronged shareholders to enforce the observance of the veto. This is a somewhat difficult case because it appears to suggest that only membership rights as such can be enforced. The reconciliation of this difficulty lies in saying that the membership rights of a shareholder include the right to have the articles observed, and this right may be enforced even where it leads indirectly to the enforcement of an outsider right, as in this case. Of course this significantly widens the scope of the s14 contract, and it is by no means clear that *Salmon* v *Quin & Axtens* is correctly decided. At some future date a court may have to resolve these uncertainties about the scope of s14 and about the capacities in which the parties to this deemed contract appear. Until then, this argument must at least be a plausible one, and James would be well advised to try it.

The articles give the directors an absolute power to refuse to register a transfer, so James's only hope of success on this point would be to show that the directors were acting mala fides, which is always difficult to prove. A different approach to the problem would be to petition under CA 1985 s459 on the grounds that the affairs of the company were being conducted in a manner unfairly prejudicial to some part of the membership. However, this section is limited to matters affecting the petitioner as a member, and the question of the directorship does not appear to qualify. The effect of the directors' conduct on the value of James's shares would clearly qualify under s459. It may be observed that the prejudice suffered must be 'unfair', but there seems to be a good argument for saying that this requirement is satisfied here. Section 459 seems to be more liberal to dissentient shareholders than the old s210, under which it was very nearly impossible to launch a successful petition, and James would have a reasonable chance in this case of securing a court order that his shares be bought out at proper market value.

The final option would be to petition under IA 1986 s122 for the winding up of the company on the grounds that this would be just and equitable. This remedy may be available in small companies (sometimes referred to as quasi-partnerships) where the necessary relationship of trust among the participants has collapsed - *Ebrahimi* v *Westbourne Galleries Ltd* (1973) - and there is some evidence that this has happened here. James has some prospect of success under this section, though the courts are generally reluctant to order so drastic a remedy. It is also open to question whether James really wants the company wound up - he is unlikely to do so well financially from this as he would from the alternative of an order for the buying out of his shares.

Tutorial comment

The above answer illustrates the difficulty of separating the parts of an answer like this: the issues as to the membership rights and the transfer of shares are closely related to the possibility of actions under s459 or s122. However, for ease of reference, the other questions in this chapter concentrate heavily on the minority oppression aspects. In some instances (which are noted in the text) the question re-appears in another chapter with the emphasis on other aspects.

QUESTION 2

Andrew and Henry who had conducted a partnership called Harryandy's Fish and Chips decided to continue their business through a limited company. They each subscribed for 100 £1 shares and informally agreed that each would be chairman for a year and that the chairman's casting vote at general meetings conferred by Regulation 50 of Table A, would never be exercised. At the Annual General Meeting in 1984, Andrew - who was the chairman that year - proposed that his son John be appointed to the board and that 10 shares be issued to him. Henry refused, but Andrew purported to use the casting vote conferred on the chairman and declared the resolution carried.

Henry immediately started proceedings for the winding up of the company on the grounds of deadlock, whereupon Andrew and John voted in favour of a resolution removing Henry from the board of directors.

Discuss.

University of London LLB Examination
(for External Students) Company Law June 1986 Q8

General comment

This is a question which is heavily slanted towards minority protection, though a few other areas are covered in passing. The following deals with the minority protection aspects, with cross-references to the other topics.

Skeleton solution

Company is a 'quasi-partnership' so members must deal fairly with each other. Agreement as to chairmanship is valid and binding. H can petition under IA s122 for winding-up on ground of deadlock, but this is an extreme solution. Alternatively he may use CA s459 to restrain conduct of majority.

Suggested solution

Andrew and Henry have formed a company from what was previously a partnership. Prima facie the company has the characteristics of a quasi-partnership, as explained by Lord Wilberforce in *Ebrahimi* v *Westbourne Galleries* (1973), namely that it was formed on the basis of a personal relationship between the participants, that there is an understanding that each of the participants will be concerned in the management of the business and that there is a restriction on the transfer of shares. Although the term 'quasi-partnership' is commonly used, it must be remembered that this is still a limited company. Where the relationship of trust which is the basis of the company has broken down it may be appropriate to make a winding-up order under the 'just and equitable' ground in Insolvency Act 1986 s122. This ground necessarily confers a very wide and general discretion upon the court. In the present case the shareholders have unanimously agreed that one person would be chairman for the year and that the chairman's casting vote would not have effect. This is a valid agreement to alter the articles, notwithstanding the absence of any formal resolution: *Re Duomatic* (1969); *Re Bailey, Hay & Co Ltd* (1971). Thus the vote purportedly cast by Andrew to ensure his son's appointment to the Board is invalid.

[The question of the issue of shares should also be dealt with here - see chapter 7.]

In *Ebrahimi* v *Westbourne Galleries* the plaintiff was removed from the board of a quasi-partnership and found himself locked into the company because he could not dispose of his shares. A similar situation occurs here, as Henry has presumably been removed under s303 after complaining of deadlock. This would give Henry worthwhile ammunition for beginning a s122 petition. Success is not guaranteed, however, for the courts are reluctant to order the drastic remedy of winding up a solvent and viable company. A less drastic, and perhaps more attractive, alternative would be for Henry to seek an order under Companies Act (CA) 1985 s459 that the majority buy out his shareholding. In order to be eligible for this Henry would have to show that the affairs of the company were being conducted in a manner unfairly prejudicial to some part of the membership (in this case himself). This provision, which in 1980 replaced the old CA 1948 s210, is thought to be more liberal than the former provision and to give the court more scope. Authorities on his section show that in cases of this kind the court may well be prepared to make a s459 order even where a s122 winding up will be refused. It is consequently thought that this offers Henry's best hope of a satisfactory resolution to the dispute.

Tutorial comment

It is instructive to contrast with question 2 above with question 1 in chapter 12. This is a question which is primarily about the breach of directors' duties, but where the topic is presented in the form of an instruction to advise a minority shareholder who has discovered the breaches of duty. Comparison of the two questions will show the importance of deciding what the examiner is really asking for - question 1 chapter 12 looks at first sight as if it is about minority protection, but in fact the emphasis is on directors' duties, and it is for that reason that it has been placed in chapter 12.

A similar point may be made about question 1, chapter 7, which primarily relates to the issue of shares, but also has a point in it about a disgruntled minority shareholder. See chapter 7 for a suggested solution to this problem.

Question 2 in chapter 12 is an example of a problem where minority protection occurs even more peripherally. The question is clearly primarily concerned with removal of directors, but a full answer also needs to consider the risk that the director who is to be removed will seek some form of minority protection.

Another difficulty for students is that minority protection can often appear in a question which appears at first sight to be mainly about directors' duties. The next set of problems are all alluded to in chapter 12, and students may be surprised to find them included in the chapter on minority protection. As the suggested answers show, a good attempt at these questions needs to concentrate heavily on the protection of minorities.

QUESTION 3

Vegeteria plc is a company specialising in the growth and sale of vegetables. Keith, Jane and Richard are the three directors of the company. They each have 5,000 shares. The company has issued a further 10,000 shares. All shares have one vote per share. Keith always votes as Jane wishes. Richard wishes to diversify the business of the company and to commence growing flowers on a large scale. This would be intra vires, but Jane disagrees and Richard is continually outvoted. Richard takes advantage of a time when Keith and Jane are on holiday and begins to set up a flower growing business in the name of the company. He also acquires 5,000 shares from some of the minority shareholders who wished to dispose of their interest in the company. When Keith and Jane returned they were determined to prevent this happening again and at a duly convened directors' meeting issued 10,000 shares to Victoria, their daughter, at par. At the annual general meeting of the company they asserted that the company needed more capital and on this basis the issue of the shares to Victoria was approved. Although Victoria did not vote, Keith and Jane voted for the resolution approving the issue, Richard voted against, but Keith, as chairman, used his casting vote to pass the resolution. A resolution to remove Richard from the Board of Directors was passed in the same way.

Advise Richard.

University of London LLB Examination
(for External Students) Company Law June 1984 Q4

General comment

A number of topics are covered here, including the issuing of shares (chapter 7) and voting at General Meetings (chapter 11). The following solution, which deals only with the essential impropriety of the resolution (see chapters 7 and 11 for other aspects of the problem) will serve well as a suggested solution for any problem question where it is desired to overturn a company resolution.

Skeleton solution

Resolutions may be challenged for lack of bona fides, but the law here is uncertain.

Alternatively K may use IA s122 or CA s459. The former is probably too drastic in case of a public company, but the latter may well be appropriate.

Suggested solution

Any resolution can be challenged on the ground that it was not passed bona fide for the benefit of the company as a whole. The difficulty is to determine what this phrase means and to establish in what cases the court will be prepared to upset the decision of the majority. In *Greenhalgh* v *Arderne Cinemas* (1946) it was stated that the test is to be applied by finding a hypothetical individual shareholder and enquiring whether the resolution was for his benefit. The problem is of course that this hypothetical shareholder by definition does not exist. An alternative approach is to ask whether the resolution discriminates between the majority and the minority. In this form the test is surely much too wide - it comes close to giving the minority a veto on anything the majority may do; a modified version would ask whether the resolution discriminated unfairly, but this involves a substantial value judgment and raises the whole question of the extent to which the court should be prepared to modify the general principle of majority rule. It is clear that, at any rate in small companies, the majority cannot act in complete disregard of the interests of the minority. What is not clear is the extent of the protection which the law grants to the minority, and this fact makes it very difficult to give emphatic advice in the present case. It can perhaps be said that the resolution of the majority will be accepted by the court at face value unless there are suspicious circumstances: *Shuttleworth* v *Cox Bros & Co (Maidenhead) Ltd* (1927); *Sidebotham* v *Kershaw, Leese & Co* (1920).

Keith's other avenues of approach would appear to lie under Companies Act 1985 s459 and/or Insolvency Act 1986 s122. The latter, involving the drastic remedy of winding up the company, is probably not appropriate in a public company, even one which has only a small number of shareholders. Section 459 may offer some prospect of success - it is at least arguable that the conduct of the affairs of the company has been unfairly prejudicial to Richard, but in the case of a public company it must again be questioned whether the court would be willing to make an order requiring the re-instatement of a director or determining which business the company should/should not pursue.

QUESTION 4

Irene, Jill and Kate are directors of Seaside Ltd which arranges British seaside holidays, specialising in holidays where children would be welcome, although the objects of the company are wide enough to enable it to deal in any type of holiday. Irene and Jill each hold 30% of the shares in the company. The remaining 40% is held by Kate. All the directors are active in the running of the business and the profits are distributed mainly in the form of director's renumeration, rather then as dividends. Kate attended all meetings in which policy was formed and often suggested new ideas for company development. She was, therefore, surprised to learn that Irene and Jill booked a trip for themselves to Antarctica, paid for the trip out of company funds, describing it in a document sent to 'all shareholders' as a 'research trip'.

On their return from the trip Irene and Jill refused to allow Kate to take part in any company decisions and refused to repay any of the money spent on the trip. Kate fears that the company is now unable to pay its debts as they fall due and consults you for advice.

Advise Kate.

University of London LLB Examination
(for External Students) Company Law June 1988 Q7

General comment

In the 1988 paper this area was paired, unusually, with that of wrongful and fraudulent trading. These latter topics are examined in chapter 10, and the following answer concentrates on the minority protection aspects of the question.

Skeleton solution

Quasi-partnership - exclusions from management - winding-up under IA s122 - possibly too drastic - CA s459 petition preferable - order for purchase of shares - derivative action possible but less satisfactory.

Suggested solution

The company here has three shareholders. All are directors and all are actively engaged in the running of the business. This is very similar to the 'quasi-partnership' arrangement found in *Ebrahimi* v *Westbourne Galleries* (1973) in that all participate in management and the profit is distributed as remuneration rather than as dividend. By contrast with *Ebrahimi*, though, there is no evidence of a clause restricting the transfer of shares, nor has there been any refusal to pay the aggrieved shareholder. She has been excluded from decision-making in the company and the others have made decisions about the trip to Antarctica without consulting Kate. The exclusion from management is probably Kate's strongest argument for a winding-up order under

Insolvency Act s122 - this was the ground on which the petition ultimately succeeded in *Ebrahimi*.

It must be borne in mind, though, that Kate will not necessarily want the drastic remedy of a winding-up; she may prefer to keep the company going but subject to some sensible regulation of the unacceptable behaviour of the majority. In this case a more appropriate solution for her would be to present a petition under Companies Act (CA) 1985 s459 complaining that the affairs of the company are being conducted in a way which is unfairly prejudicial to her. This section, which appears to be more liberal in its effect than the former, highly restrictive CA 1948 s210, allows the court to make virtually any order it thinks fit. A common order is that the majority buy the petitioner's shares at a fair value, and this is likely to suit Kate here, since the company is not doing well - she will be particularly satisfied if she can get her shares purchased at the price which prevailed before the conduct complained of.

Kate may also be able to bring a derivative action for the fraud on the minority which the majority have apparently committed by misappropriating company funds for the Antarctica trip, but in practice a petition under s459 is likely to achieve much the same effect more easily.

[For the wrongful trading aspects of this question see Chapter 10].

QUESTION 5

'Despite many attempts by the legislature, no effective statutory remedy to safeguard the interests of minority shareholders has [been] or will be developed.' Discuss.

University of London LLB Examination
(for External Students) Company Law June 1985 Q1

General comment

It is exceptional for the topic of minority protection to appear as an essay question.

Some care is needed in dealing with this question. First, it asks about statutory remedies; thus, the *Foss* v *Harbottle* (1843) line of cases, which relate to a form of protection offered at common law, are not relevant (for an essay on this area see below). Secondly, the question refers to successive attempts by the legislature, and students therefore need to deal with the various provisions which have been enacted over the years, in addition to the present law.

Skeleton solution

Main provisions are CA 1985 s459 and IA 1986 s122.

Section 459 gives court wide discretion, especially to order buy-out of shares - s459 more liberal than old s210 - now provides most effective and commonly-used remedy.

Section 122 is more drastic - various established situations for using it - especially quasi-partnership.

Question depends on how much protection is thought fair for minority shareholder - note general principle of majority rule.

Suggested solution

Traditionally, relief has been afforded to the minority shareholder through two main routes. The first is the petition under Companies Act (CA) 1985 s459 (formerly CA 1980, replacing CA 1948 s210); the second is the winding-up petition under Insolvency Act (IA) 1986 s122 (formerly CA 1948 s222, then CA 1985 s517).

Section 459 by its terms allows the court to make a wide variety of orders in favour of the minority shareholder, including in particular the buying out of the shares of the dissentient minority. The practical effectiveness of this remedy depends, however, on the attitude of the courts. This has to be understood in the light of the history of s459. It was enacted in 1980 to replace the former s210, which had proved very unsatisfactory because of the need for a course of conduct rather than isolated acts of oppression ('oppression' was defined by Lord Simonds in *Scottish Cooperative Welfare Society (SCWS)* v *Meyer* (1959) as 'harsh, burdensome and/or wrongful conduct', which placed a heavy burden of proof on petitioners) and because it was necessary to show that the facts would have justified a winding-up petition on the just and equitable ground. In view of this it is not surprising that there were only two successful petitions under s210: *SCWS* v *Meyer* and *Re HR Harmar Ltd* (1959). The wording of s459 is more liberal, and the courts have interpreted it in a less restrictive way; thus, there is no requirement that the conduct be such as would justify a winding-up order: *Re London School of Electronics* (1986). A single act or omission can justify a petition, and s459 refers to 'unfair prejudice' rather than 'oppression', which appears to be a less onerous test (*Re a Company* (1983)) though it is difficult to say how much less onerous. Many of the s459 cases have concerned the valuation of shares for buy-out purposes (eg *Re OC Transport Services Ltd* (1984)). Relief under s459 is discretionary, and the court will expect the petitioner to come to court with clean hands: *Re Bird Precision Bellows Ltd* (1984), *Nurcombe* v *Nurcombe* (1984).

However, one restriction imposed by the old s210 is unchanged. It appears that the petitioner must still be affected in his position as member; thus, the removal of a director from office will not of itself entitle that director to bring a s210 petition, even if he is a member. This rule has been criticised, but it is submitted that it is perfectly justified; s210 is aimed at shareholder rights, and it would be invidious if a sacked director who is a shareholder were in a better position than one who is not a member.

Under IA s122 the court may order a winding-up of the company on the ground that it is 'just and equitable' to do so. Again, this gives the court a very wide discretion, but it is to be noted that there is only one remedy available under this provision, and that it is a drastic one. There are a few established categories of case where this relief is available: loss of confidence between the participants - *Loch* v *Blackwood Ltd* (1924); deadlock - *Re Bondi Better Bananas Ltd* (1952); failure of the substratum - *Re German Date Coffee Ltd* (1882). However, the leading case in this area, *Ebrahimi* v *Westbourne Galleries Ltd* (1973), shows that the discretion goes much wider than this. Where there is a special underlying obligation between the members that so long as the business continues each will be entitled to management participation, then it will be proper to subject the exercise of legal rights (such as removal of a director under CA 1985 s303) to equitable considerations, and a breach of the equitable obligations thereby arising may be sufficient grounds for a winding-up under s122. The kind of company where this principle will be invoked is likely to share certain of the characteristics of Westbourne Galleries Ltd eg that there is a personal relationship between the parties, that there is an understanding with regard to management and that there is a restriction on the transfer of shares. In these circumstances s122 is a potent weapon in the hands of a minority shareholder, though it is fair to say that the courts are reluctant to order the winding-up of a viable company and may prefer to make a buy-out order under s459.

In extreme cases it may be possible to bring a misfeasance action against a director or even to obtain a DTI investigation under CA 1985 s431 et seq, but these remedies are in practice confined to large public companies.

The question asks whether these remedies are effective to protect the minority shareholder. It must be understood that there can never be an automatic remedy for a disgruntled shareholder (it cannot simply be assumed that he is in the right). Company law operates on the principle of majority rule, and the only workable solution is to allow that majority rule to prevail in the great majority of cases. The present scheme, whereby the court is given a wide discretion and is then left to arbitrate on the merits of particular cases, is probably the best which can be devised, though it is arguable that s459 is still a little too restrictive.

Tutorial comment

The questions dealt with above cover most of the major aspects of minority protection. The most important omission concerns the rule in *Foss* v *Harbottle* (1843) and the exceptions to it. The topic is well-suited to an essay question, such as that given below.

QUESTION 6

How important are the exceptions to the rule in *Foss* v *Harbottle* in protecting the minority shareholder from oppressive conduct by the majority?

Written by Editor
September 1989

General comment

This question is not taken from a London LLB External paper. In dealing with it students need to be aware that there are two matters to consider. The first is to identify properly the rule and the exceptions to it; the second is to place these exceptions in their proper context with regard to the protection of minorities. This naturally involves considering other remedies available, but the examination of these must not be allowed to dominate the answer.

Skeleton solution

General rule: company (not shareholders) must sue for a wrong done to the company.

Exceptions: fraud on minority (but scope of this is vague); illegal acts by company; failure to get correct majority; breach of membership rights. These are of limited value.

Note also statutory exceptions, especially CA 1985 s459 and IA 1986 s122.

Suggested solution

The rule in *Foss* v *Harbottle* (1843) may be summarised as being that where a wrong is done to the company in the form of a breach of the duty owed to it by its directors, the proper plaintiff in an action for that wrong is the company itself and not any of the shareholders. There are, however, limited exceptions to that rule, which may help the minority of shareholders in a number of situations.

Perhaps the most important example arises where the conduct of the wrongdoers amounts to a fraud on the minority. In such cases the aggrieved minority may sue in their own name. The ambit of this exception was considered at length in *Prudential Assurance Co Ltd* v *Newman Industries Ltd* (1980) but it is not possible to be more precise than to say that the allowing of such an action lies in the discretion of the court. Actions in the names of the shareholders will also be permitted in the case of ultra vires or illegal acts, since these are not capable of ratification. In *Cotter* v *National Union of Seamen* (1929) it was held that a further exception existed where the act complained of required a special majority but had only received an ordinary majority. The same principle applies where the member complains of a breach of his membership rights (ie the contract under Companies Act (CA) 1985 s14) since in this event there can be no argument that the company is the proper plaintiff.

It can be seen that the exceptions to the rule in *Foss* v *Harbottle* are all significant within their own limited spheres. However, it should also be clear that they fail to address a number of the significant problems of company law and the protection of minorities. It is very easy for the majority to oppress the minority (and to have their actions approved by the General Meeting) without falling within any of the exceptions mentioned. In view of this it is necessary to mention at least briefly some of the other ways in which minorities can be protected.

By far the most important of these at the present day is CA 1985 s459. This applies where the affairs of a company are being conducted in a manner unfairly prejudicial to some part of the membership. It gives the court very wide powers to grant relief to the minority shareholders. The most important options available are the making of an order requiring the discontinuance of a particular course of conduct and the making of an order requiring the majority to buy out the shares of the minority at a fair price.

A more drastic remedy which is also available is a winding-up order under Insolvency Act (IA) 1986 s122 on the ground that winding-up is just and equitable. This is most commonly used in cases of quasi-partnerships, where the majority are unfairly excluding the minority from participation in management: see *Ebrahimi* v *Westbourne Galleries* (1973). Although this remedy may sometimes be helpful, it must be remembered that it is by its nature a drastic one, and it should therefore not be sought lightly.

These two sections (CA s459 and IA s122) are in practical terms far more commonly used than are the exceptions to *Foss* v *Harbottle*, and it can legitimately be said that these exceptions play only a small part in the modern protection of minority shareholders.

14   COMPANY INVESTIGATIONS

14.1   Introduction

14.2   Key points

14.3   Analysis of questions

14.4   Questions

14.1   Introduction

To some extent this topic can be seen as overlapping with that of minority protection, since seeking an investigation into the company's affairs is one of the ways in which a disaffected minority can protect itself. Investigations are, however, a relatively minor part of that topic, since minorities now have more effective means of protection available to them. Further, investigations arise in circumstances other than that of a disaffected minority, and are worthy of independent treatment.

14.2   Key points

a)   *Source of powers*

The power of the Secretary of State to order an investigation into the affairs of a company is found in Part XIV of the Companies Act 1985. This Part also contains powers relating to the investigation of company ownership and of dealings in the shares of a company.

b)   *Investigation of affairs*

Sections 431-441 of the 1985 Act deal with general investigations into a company's affairs, which may be ordered on the application of the members of the company. The inspectors appointed by the Secretary of State have very wide powers to take evidence and to call for the production of documents (ss433-435). It is a contempt of court to obstruct such an investigation (s436).

At the conclusion of the investigation (and at intervals during it if so required by the Secretary of State) the inspectors must submit a report to the Secretary of State.

As a result of the report the Secretary of State may authorise any person to bring civil proceedings in the name of the company (s438) or may present a petition for the winding-up of the company (s440).

c)   *Investigations of ownership*

Sections 442-446 contain powers relating to the appointment of inspectors to investigate the ownership of shares in a company. Such investigations are governed by the same rules as apply to investigations under ss431-441, with the additional provision (s445) that in case of difficulty in discovering the facts about the ownership of the shares the Secretary of State may supend the voting and dividend rights attaching to the shares.

d)   *Investigations of share dealings*

Under s447 an investigation may be ordered where it appears that there may have been improper dealings in a company's shares by any director or by a person connected with a director of the company. Once again the procedural and penal provisions of ss431-441 apply to such investigations.

e)   *Value of Part XIV*

Part XIV is now used quite often in large public companies. However, it remains difficult to acquire the necessary information and the investigation is inevitably a slow process.

In the context of private companies these provisions seem largely irrelevant, since other forms of minority protection (especially CA 1985 s459) are usually much more appropriate and convenient.

14.3   Analysis of questions

This is in some ways a rather obscure topic, and one which relatively few students are likely to prepare. Nevertheless it has occurred twice on the London LLB External paper since 1983, and is worthy of some attention.

The topic has always arisen in essay form, and it is likely that it will continue to do so; in view of the other forms of protection available it would be a very contrived problem question in which the bulk of the answer was concerned with company investigations.

14.4   Questions

The two questions which have been set on this topic are printed below. It can be seen that both run along very much the same lines, asking about two matters, the adequacy of the powers in a legal sense and the strength of the political will to use those powers. The suggested essay which appears below the questions would do equally well for either question and, it is thought, for any other essay question on this topic which is likely to appear. It may be observed in passing that students who are not well versed in the relevant legislation would be well advised to steer clear of this topic if at all possible - this is not an area in which intelligent students can bluff their way through.

QUESTIONS

'Although the investigative powers of the Department of Trade have been substantially extended by recent legislation, that Department still lacks both the powers and the will to act as a watchdog for minority shareholders.' Discuss.

University of London LLB Examination
(for External Students) Company Law June 1984 Q3

'Statute has now provided sufficient machinery for any type of corporate investigation which may be necessary. What is lacking is the will to use that machinery.' Discuss.

University of London LLB Examination
(for External Students) Company Law June 1987 Q1(a)

Skeleton solution

Powers contained in CA 1985 Part XIV.

Appointments of inspectors to investigate and report. Secretary of State may act on their report.

Investigations into company ownership and dealings in shares. Petitions to wind-up company.

Powers are extensive - major problem seems to be reluctance to use them in practice.

Suggested solution

One of the duties of the Secretary of State is to ensure that companies conduct their affairs in an appropriate manner and that the interests of creditors are properly protected. Part XIV of the Companies Act 1985 gives the Secretary of State considerable investigative and regulatory powers to assist him in carrying out this duty.

Under s431 of the Act the Secretary of State can appoint one or more inspectors to investigate the affairs of a company. This may be done on the application of certain interested parties or on the application of the company itself. The Secretary of State must be satisfied that there are good reasons for making the application, though the statute does not define what these reasons may include.

Under s432 the Secretary of State may appoint inspectors without the need for any application if he suspects that the company's affairs are being conducted in a manner prejudicial to the interests of creditors or if he suspects fraud. He is not subject to the rules of natural justice in deciding whether to appoint inspectors under this provision: *Norwest Holst Ltd* v *Department of Trade* (1978). Section 432 also allows the court to require the Secretary of State to appoint inspectors.

Once appointed, inspectors are given certain powers by the Act. They may require the production of documents and may take statements under oath from officers and others concerned with the running of the company. They may make interim reports to the Secretary of State and must make a final report. It is a contempt of court to obstruct the inspectors in their enquiries. Once the report is made the Secretary of State may take civil proceedings on behalf of the company if he judges it expedient to do so - s438.

In addition to the above the Secretary of State has the power to order investigations into company ownership (s442) and into dealings in the shares of a company (s449). These powers are supplemented by powers to enter and search premises (s448) and require production of documents (s447). It is a criminal offence to destroy relevant documents in such cases (s450).

In practice the inspector has to work on his own initiative, and the success of the investigation will depend heavily on the energy and perseverance which he brings to his task - see, for example, *Re Pergamon Press* (1971) and *Maxwell* v *Department of Trade* (1974).

Finally, the Secretary of State may petition for the winding-up of the company under Insolvency Act s122 on the just and equitable ground and can apply for a disqualification order against a director or shadow director of a company under s8 and sch 1, Company Directors Disqualification Act 1986.

The above clearly indicates that a wide range of powers is available, and recent years have seen an increased willingness to exercise those powers, especially in cases such as the Guinness scandal, which attract considerable public interest. The major difficulty seems to be that there is a reluctance to take legal proceedings against those involved in running the company, even when the inspector's report points clearly to serious wrongdoing. It is at this latter point that the regulatory system seems to break down; no change in the law can remedy this, since it is a political issue rather than a legal one.

15   INDUSTRIAL DEMOCRACY

15.1   Introduction

15.2   Key points

15.3   Analysis of questions

15.4   Questions

15.1   Introduction

This chapter deals with the topic of industrial democracy, and in particular with the proposals for reform of the law contained in the Report of the Committee of Inquiry into Industrial Democracy (Cmnd 6706), known as the Bullock Report.

15.2   Key points

a)   *The present law*

There is at present no statutory requirement for workers to be represented in the managerial structure of a company, and it is rare in practice for them to have any representation at board level. Their interests are protected, if at all, only through trade union representation.

b)   *The proposals*

The Bullock Report recommended that there should be a system of worker-directors in all companies employing more than 2,000 people. These directors would be appointed by the workforce and would be removable by them. It would be their duty to represent at board level the interests of the workers.

c)   *The difficulties*

Industrialists have objected to the principle of worker-directors, alleging that workers have neither the expertise nor the interest to become directors and have control over the fate of the company. This is an essentially ideological argument, and one which is very difficult to answer in the absence of rather better empirical evidence than is at present available.

From a legal point of view a more intractable problem is that of determining the role and duties of the proposed worker-directors. At present directors owe their duty to the company, rather than to the shareholders, notwithstanding that they are appointed by the latter. It is unclear whether the same would apply to worker-directors, though the imposition of such a rule would do much to defeat the purpose of introducing the scheme in the first place.

A related difficulty concerns the relationship between the board of directors and the general meeting. At present the latter has at least some control over the former, though it is a matter of dispute to what extent the powers of the GM are effectively delegated to the board. This confusion is likely to increase if worker-directors are added to the board.

d) *The prospects*

At present there seems no practical likelihood that these proposals will be implemented. It should be noted, though, that the adoption by the EEC of the Social Charter appears to bring the prospect of worker participation somewhat nearer, and that the proposed regimes for the European Company will all involve some form of worker paticipation.

15.3 Analysis of questions

This topic has appeared four times since 1983 on the London LLB external paper. Each time it has been an essay question; indeed, it is difficult to see how a problem question could sensibly be set, since the ideas under discussion are no more than proposals, which have not been implemented, and at the present time have no great prospect of being implemented. The four questions are set out below, and it can readily be seen that they are merely four different versions of the same basic question; although the 1988 question may at first sight look somewhat different in that it is limited to public companies, it must be remembered that the Bullock proposals were only intended to apply to companies employing at least 2,000 people, which would rule out private companies. Also, in private companies the directors and shareholders are commonly the same people, so that the issue does not arise in the same form. It is therefore suggested that the essay set out below the questions will serve perfectly well as an answer to any of these questions and for that matter to any essay question which is likely to be set on industrial democracy.

It is important to note, however, that all these questions go beyond merely asking for an evaluation of the Bullock proposals. All ask about the ways in which company law would need to be modified in order to deal with worker directors. This issue principally concerns the relationship between the directors and the shareholders, and thus involves article 80 of Table A. A good answer to the question must therefore deal adequately with this point.

15.4 Questions

QUESTIONS

'When proposals that boards of directors of companies must contain representatives of employees are enacted, the law will have to define, more carefully than it does at present, the relationship between boards and the shareholders in general meeting. If employee directors are to have a share in real power, they cannot be subjected to the ultimate control of the shareholders.' Discuss.

University of London LLB Examination
(for External Students) Company Law June 1983 Q2

'If the Bullock proposals to have equal representation of shareholders and employees on the Board of Directors were enacted, radical alterations to fundamental company law principles would have to be undertaken.' Discuss.

University of London LLB Examination
(for External Students) Company Law June 1984 Q2

'The power of the board of directors has grown as the general meeting of shareholders has become weaker. Were the Bullock Committee proposals to be enacted, this would strengthen the board of directors yet further.' Discuss.

University of London LLB Examination
(for External Students) Company Law June 1986 Q3

Consider the arguments in favour of and against representation of the employees of large public companies on the board of directors. What, if any, would be the effect of such representation on the legal principles governing directors' fiduciary duties.

University of London LLB Examination
(for External Students) Company Law June 1988 Q2

Skeleton solution

Bullock Committee wanted compulsory representation in larger companies. This is very controversial - substantial political opposition.

Implementation of proposals requires consideration of relationship between board and GM - can GM take back powers delegated to board?; also needs consideration of worker-directors' duties - owed to company or to fellow employees.

Suggested solution

It is appropriate to begin by summarising the recommendations of the Bullock Committee. The majority of the Committee favoured the introduction of so-called 'worker-directors', ie directors chosen from among the workforce and appointed to represent their interests at Board level. The Report recognised that in practice it is the Board which makes all the important financial and managerial decisions, notwithstanding that in theory these are reserved to the shareholders in General Meeting. The Report wanted to recognise this fact by allowing representation of the workers at board level in groups of companies as well as in individual companies with at least 2,000 employees. There would be an equal number of non-worker directors and worker-directors plus a third group of directors appointed jointly by the other two groups, though this third group would be smaller than either of the other two.

It is fair to say that the proposals proved very controversial. A minority report from the Committee was opposed to parity of representation, whilst accepting the principle of worker-directors. Others have suggested a two-tier Board structure such as operates in some other EEC countries, whilst some industrialists criticised the Committee's terms of reference for assuming that there should be worker-directors. The present government is adamantly opposed to the idea of worker directors, though there is likely to be continued pressure from the EEC for a move in this direction. It may be noted in passing that the European Commission's proposals for a European Company

Statute have repeatedly foundered on the UK's opposition to the proposals for compulsory worker participation.

What if the proposals were to be implemented? Modern company law does not determine with any clarity the relationship between the board and the shareholders. Generally the rule is that the shareholders are supreme, but may delegate their powers to the board. Article 80 of Table A effects a fairly wide delegation, and in practice it seems that the vast majority of the decisions are made by the board (of course in small companies the board and the shareholders may well be the same people). What is unclear is whether the shareholders, having delegated by article 80, are then entitled to interfere in the board's decisions. One view assumes that there is a contractual delegation which the members cannot revoke. This view is supported by cases such as *Scott* v *Scott* (1943), *Gramophone & Typewriter Co Ltd* v *Stanley* (1908), *Salmon* v *Quin & Axtens* (1909). The minority view is that the directors are agents of the shareholders who, as principals, can intervene at any time. *Marshall's Valve Gear Co Ltd* v *Manning Wardle* (1909) (General Meeting entitled to institute proceedings in the company's name if directors unwilling) is perhaps the best authority for this view. At a semantic level the problem is that the reference in article 80 to the Regulations appears self-contradictory, as Lord Clauson pointed out in *Scott* v *Scott*. *Alexander Ward & Co* v *Samyang Navigation Co Ltd* (1975) suggests a possible reconciliation, namely that the board and the GM have parallel authority, but this still leaves a problem of what happens if they disagree. The law on this point is by no means resolved, though it is submitted that the principal/agent analysis is the correct one. What is clear, however, is that the presence of worker-directors not appointed by the shareholders would require some decision to be made on the position of the board, since conflicts become all the more likely. A related problem is to know to whom the directors are to be answerable. One solution is that each director is responsible to the group which appointed him, and this may be the only option, since it is to be presumed that a director can be removed from office only by the group which appointed him. If the shareholders are given the power to overrule the board (including the worker-directors) the question will be asked, why the workers cannot do the same. It can therefore safely be said that the enactment of these proposals will necessitate decisions about some fundamental concepts of company law.

16   INSIDER DEALING

16.1   Introduction

16.2   Key points

16.3   Recent cases and statutes

16.4   Analysis of questions

16.5   Questions

16.1   Introduction

This chapter deals with the situation where a person who is in possession of unpublished price-sensitive information about a company uses that information to deal in the securities of that company so as to make a profit for himself. In some circumstances this is a criminal offence under the Company Securities (Insider Dealing) Act 1985.

16.2   Key points

a)   *Definition*

Insider trading arises when a person wrongfully uses unpublished price-sensitive information about a company as the basis for dealing in the shares of that company.

b)   *Policy arguments*

It is a matter of some dispute whether the law should act to prohibit insider dealing. According to one view this is a 'victimless crime', whilst another view is that the timely exploitation of information is what the Stock Market is all about. The argument on the other side is that it is necessary to protect small investors who do not have access to inside information, and that it is necessary to preserve public confidence in the integrity of the market generally by prohibiting practices of this kind. At the present day the arguments in favour of prohibition are in the ascendancy.

c)   *To whom the prohibition applies*

There are four categories of persons to whom the prohibition may apply. They are: individuals connected with a company, persons contemplating a takeover of a company, public servants and tippees (ie persons not in any of the above categories but who have obtained their information from a person connected with the company).

The principal example of a person connected with a company is a director or officer of the company. But the term also extends to directors and officers of any connected company and to the company's professional advisers.

As regards contemplated take-overs the prohibition applies only where the person contemplating the take-over knows that this fact is itself price-sensitive information.

Public servants (including all civil servants and the employees of all the self-regulating organisations (SROs) under the Financial Services Act 1986) also come within the prohibition.

There is a further requirement that the person who has the information must have it in such circumstances that it would be reasonable to expect him not to disclose it. At present it is unclear what this means.

d) *The nature of the prohibition*

A person who is caught by one of the prohibitions outlined above is forbidden to deal in the securities of the company concerned for a period of six months after acquiring the information. This time limit was set on the basis that after six months it was likely that the information would have ceased to be sufficiently up to date to be significantly price-sensitive.

e) *The sanction*

Insider dealing is a criminal offence, punishable with an unlimited fine and/or imprisonment for up to seven years. So far no one has ever served a prison sentence for it in this country.

16.3   Recent cases and statutes

Company Securities (Insider Dealing) Act 1985. This is the statute which imposes criminal penalties for insider dealing.

R v *Fisher* (1988) 4 BCC 360 considers the meaning of 'obtaining' information, and whether information can be said to be 'obtained' when a person receives it without any positive effort on his part, as for example by overhearing it.

16.4   Analysis of questions

Insider dealing is an extremely topical subject, which has attracted substantial media comment and a few cases. It has appeared in two problem questions on the London LLB External paper since 1983, once as the major part of a question, once as a rather smaller part of a question. It is also very well suited to an essay question, and a suggested solution to a standard essay on this topic is therefore included in this chapter. The statutory developments in this field have happened in the past decade, but there is still a grave shortage of reported cases. Students who contemplate attempting questions in this area would do well to have at least some familiarity with insider dealing 'scandals', such as the Guinness takeover, which have received a lot of publicity, even though the legal issues connected with them have not yet been resolved. It should also be pointed out that this is another somewhat specialist area with detailed technical rules. Students who try to bluff their way through without knowing those rules take a very grave risk.

16.5   Questions

QUESTION 1

Toucan plc is a large public company. Three of its directors are Cedric, John and Bill. Each holds 5,000 £1 shares. Cedric discovers from Pete (a director of Distilation plc) that Distilation plc is likely soon to make a generous offer for the shares of Toucan plc in order to effect a takeover. Cedric passes on this information to John and Bill and all three borrow money from Toucan plc to buy themselves more shares in that company.

John is worried about the effect that the impending takeover will have on the value of his wife's holding in a rival company. He suggests to his wife that she should pay for their annual holiday not from their savings account as she usually did, but by selling her shares in the rival company.

The loan from the company to John, Bill and Cedric comes to light and at a general meeting a motion to take legal proceedings against them is defeated only by the votes of John, Bill, Cedric and one other director, who himself authorised the loan.

Adrian has a small shareholding in Toucan plc, is disgusted by the behaviour of the directors and asks you if there is any legal action he can take. You are asked to advise on the possible civil and criminal liability of Cedric, John, Bill and Pete.

University of London LLB Examination
(for External Students) Company Law June 1987 Q8

General' comment

This first question deals mainly with the Company Securities (Insider Dealing) Act 1985, though the provisions of CA 1985 relating to loans to directors are also of significance.

Skeleton solution

The information is clearly UPSI.

Pete: counselling and procuring (s1(7)).

Cedric: guilty because he is a 'tippee'.

John and Bill: guilty because of dealing in shares. John has also counselled and procured.

No remedy against directors, but could inform the authorities.

Loan probably void: also possible unlawful financial assistance for purchase of shares.

Suggested solution

There is no doubt that the information concerning Distillation plc's intention to take over Toucan plc would amount to unpublished price-sensitive information (UPSI) as defined by s10 of the Company Securities (Insider Dealing) Act 1985 (CS(ID)A).

Pete

If Pete deals in shares of Toucan plc (as to which the question is unclear) it is suggested that he will commit an offence under s1(2) of the Act. He passes on information to Cedric, and this would seem to give him a potential liability under s1(7) (counselling and procuring) or s1(8) (passing on UPSI). To establish this offence it must be proved that Pete knew or ought to have known that Cedric would use the information to deal or to counsel or procure others to deal.

Cedric

Cedric will probably fall foul of s1 CS(ID)A 1985: he is connected with Toucan plc and is in possession of UPSI received in consequence of that connection (s9). Under these circumstances it is an offence for him to deal in Toucan's shares or to pass the information on to another if he knows or ought to know that the other person will deal in Toucan shares. Similarly, it is an offence for him to counsel or procure any other person to deal in Toucan shares (s1(7) and (8)).

John and Bill

Under s8 both are connected with the company and therefore potentially liable under s1. In addition John may be liable under s1(7), since he appears to have counselled or procured his wife to deal in securities concerning which he was in possession of UPSI. By virtue of his connection with Toucan he acquired UPSI concerning the rival company; had he used this himself he would have been liable under s1(2).

Defences

Section 3 sets out the defences available under the Act. The only one which appears to be available on the facts given is that John may be able to claim 'avoidance of loss to another' (s3(1)(a)) as a defence to the charge under s1(7).

Adrian must be advised that the sanctions under the CS(ID)A 1985 do not extend to providing compensation for 'disgusted' shareholders and that he has no remedy against any of the directors. The position might be different if Adrian had suffered loss through the actions of the directors. Of course the company could bring actions against the miscreant directors for breach of fiduciary duty, but this does not help Adrian, since the directors' duties are not owed to the shareholders: *Percival* v *Wright* (1902); *Tett* v *Phoenix Property & Investment Co Ltd* (1985).

Borrowing

Companies Act (CA) 1985 s330 prohibits a company from lending money to its directors, except in small amounts not exceeding £2,500 in aggregate. It seems probable that in the present case the limits are exceeded. Contravention of s330 is a criminal offence by the company, and directors who permit such a contravention will also be guilty of an offence. It is submitted that the company cannot validly ratify a criminal act, so that the attempted ratification is ineffective. CA s341 provides civil remedies for breach of s330; the loan is void, and the borrower must repay the loan and account for any gains made from the money.

There would also seem to be an offence under CA s152 in that financial assistance has been given for the purpose of assisting a purchase of the company's own shares; the company and each of its officers who is in default are liable to a fine.

Tutorial comment

The other question in which the subject of insider trading has occurred on the London LLB External paper is 1983 Q5. This question is primarily concerned with directors' duties (and secondarily with minority protection). It is fully covered in chapter 12: *Directors*, question 1, to which reference should be made.

QUESTION 2

'Insider trading is a crime without a victim and the legislation prohibiting it is unduly widely drawn.' Do you agree?

Written by Editor
November 1989

General comment

Although insider trading has only so far arisen as a problem question, there is no good reason why it should not be the subject of an essay, as it is here. This question is fairly typical of the sort of essay which may be expected in this area, and the suggested solution should suffice, with only minor modifications, for virtually any essay which is set.

Skeleton solution

General ban on use of UPSI - extends to tippers - information need not have been solicited - exclusion of tippers would substantially narrow the provisions.

Insider Trading is not really victimless - seller of shares loses out - also such conduct tends to diminish confidence in the financial markets.

Suggested solution

It is necessary to begin by defining the expression 'insider trading'. This is understood to mean dealing in the securities of a company in reliance on unpublished price sensitive information about the affairs of that company. The relevant legislation is the Company Securities (Insider Dealing) Act 1985 (hereinafter referred to as 'the CS(ID)A').

The basic scheme of the CS(ID)A 1985 is to prohibit dealing based on unpublished price-sensitive information ie confidential information which is likely to affect the price of the company's shares on the open market. The prohibition applies to those who know or should have known that they were betraying a confidence in using the information. A person who is connected with a company (a director, or an employee with access to confidential information or a person connected with another company in the same group) must not, within six months of receiving the information, deal in the securities of that company, nor counsel or procure another person to do so, nor pass the information to any other person if he knows or has reason to believe that the other person will use the information to deal in the securities or to counsel or procure any other person to do so.

The Act also applies to 'tippees' ie people who have received unpublished price-sensitive information from another. A tippee is subject to the same prohibition on dealing in the securities of the company if he knows or has reasonable cause to believe that the tippor obtained the information in consequence of being connected with the company and if he (the tippee) knows that the information is unpublished price-sensitive information. It is this prohibition on dealings by tippees which has proved most controversial. In *R v Fisher* (1988) the House of Lords ruled that information could be 'obtained' by a tippee within the meaning of this prohibition even where the advice came to him unsolicited, thereby rejecting an argument which would have narrowed substantially the effective ambit of the provision.

The question suggests that the legislation is unduly widely drawn. It is hard to see how this can be so, if it is accepted that insider trading ought to be outlawed (as to which see below). To allow dealings by tippees would render the prohibitions largely nugatory, since it would be easy to evade the spirit and intention of the law by passing the information to associates.

More generally, it is suggested that insider trading is a victimless crime. This is not strictly true - the person who is induced to buy shares at an excessive price or to sell them at an inadequate price because the other party to the transaction is in possession of unpublished price sensitive information can properly be seen as the immediate victim of the insider dealing; he suffers a financial disadvantage, though it is to be observed that he has no right to compensation from the insider dealer under the Act, and it is at best doubtful whether he has any right of action at common law. However, the argument may also be put more broadly. The essential case for regulation of the financial markets is that they perform their task of helping to raise the capital necessary to enterprise more efficiently when all who deal in them can feel with reasonable confidence that the market is being conducted fairly and that they are not likely to be swindled by those who are in possession of inside information which they use for their own purposes. In this sense the market as a whole is the victim of insider trading, and it is for this reason that the prohibition on it is justified.

17   CORPORATE CRIME

17.1   Introduction

17.2   Key points

17.3   Analysis of questions

17.4   Question

17.1   Introduction

The expression 'corporate crime' relates to the question of the company's possible liability for criminal and/or tortious acts carried out on its behalf by its agents.

17.2   Key points

a)   *Criminal liability*

There is an obvious conceptual difficulty in imputing mens rea to a company, since a company does not have a mind of its own.

In practice this difficulty has been circumvented by saying that the intentions and state of mind of the controlling will of the company can be imputed to the company itself. This usually means the board of directors, though in a small company where there is a single chairman and managing director that person might be regarded as being the controlling will of the company.

There is some judicial reluctance to impose criminal liability where the act is merely that of some more junior official or employee of the company, unless of course there is a statute creating the liability which makes clear that the company is liable in such situations.

There does not appear to be any case where a company has been convicted of murder. It is often suggested that such an outcome is impossible so long as life imprisonment remains the mandatory sentence for murder - there would be some difficulty in imprisoning a company!

Occasionally the company has been able to escape liability by showing that the event in question happened due to the fault of another (including an employee). However, cases of this kind have to be treated with caution, since they appear to depend upon the availability in the particular statute of a defence couched in these terms.

b)   *Tortious liability*

It is possible for a company to owe a duty of care to another person, or indeed to another company, and there has never seemed to be any particular difficulty about holding a company liable in tort.

Two situations must be distinguished. The first is where the company is vicariously liable for the negligent act of its employee. In such cases it is not necessary that there should be any actual negligence on the part of the company, and the absence of an independent mind is therefore not an obstacle to the imposition of liability.

The second situation arises where the alleged breach of duty is by the company itself. In these cases it must be remembered that the act of the company's agents, especially the directors, can in appropriate cases be considered to be the act of the company itself.

17.3   Analysis of questions

This is a somewhat obscure topic; many company law courses ignore it entirely, but it appeared on the London LLB External in 1985, and is included for that reason. The 1985 question was an essay question, and it would seem unlikely that this topic will appear as a problem question. It is thought likely that the topic will appear by itself rather than being combined with other area of the syllabus. The question set on the 1985 paper covers the two major parts of the topic - tortious liability and criminal liability.

17.4   Question

To what extent can (a) tortious and (b) criminal liability be imposed on companies?

University of London LLB Examination
(for External Students) Company Law June 1985 Q3

General comment

This question requires examination of both the major problem areas - tort and crime.

Skeleton solution

Tort: Vicarious liability for acts of employees within scope of their employment. Also for acts of directors/managers acting in that capacity. Ultra vires acts can also be the basis of liability.

Crime: General principle is that acts of 'directing mind' of company are company's own acts. This is question of fact. Company may escape if act is through 'default of another'.

Suggested solution

It is clear that a company, like an individual, is vicariously liable for torts committed by its employees when they are acting within the scope of their employment, even if the tort includes wilful malice: *Citizens' Life Assurance Co* v *Brown* (1904). The same principle applies to criminal liability if the statute creating the liability imposes liability on employer as well as employee and the employer is a company.

In some cases the court has interpreted a statute as imposing liability on the company when the offence was committed by an officer of the company acting within the scope of his employment: *DPP* v *Kent and Sussex Contractors Ltd* (1944). More recently, though, there has been some reluctance to impose such liability unless the persons who generally manage the company have actively participated in the crime. In *Tesco Supermarkets Ltd* v *Nattrass* (1971) the company was charged under s11(2) Trades Descriptions Act 1968 with advertising goods at a lower price than that at which they were sold. The situation arose because the manager of the particular Tesco store had failed in his duty to ensure that the goods advertised were in fact available. The company had a sophisticated supervisory system designed to prevent this sort of thing from happening, but it had broken down on this occasion. Tesco pleaded that the offence was due to the default of another (the manager) and that they had taken all reasonable care. This defence is specifically allowed under the 1968 Act. The defence succeeded; Lord Reid pointed out that a company must act through living persons; in some circumstances that person is the embodiment of the company rather than its agent, and no question of vicarious liability can arise. However, it was the board of directors here which was the embodiment of the company, and its authority had not been delegated to the store manager, who was therefore to be treated as a separate person.

This case requires to be treated with some caution, for the 'default of another' defence was contained within the 1968 Act, but is not generally available to companies charged with criminal wrongdoing. The case does illustrate, however, that not every act by every junior employee will be considered to be the act of the company for the purposes of the criminal law.

Two major areas of difficulty have arisen here, and these have not so far been explored in any detail by the courts. First, for what acts of the board of directors is the company to be held responsible? So far as tort is concerned the company is responsible for the tortious acts/omissions of those who manage the company when they are acting in that capacity. In *Lennard's Carrying Co* v *Asiatic Petroleum* (1915) the company was held liable for the default of a single managing director who ought to have known that a particular ship was unseaworthy. It was said that the managing director was the directing mind and will of the company (or, as it is sometimes expressed, the company was his alter ego).

The search for the directing mind and will of the company is not restricted to looking at the formal provisions of the memorandum and articles; rather, this is a question of fact to be determined in all the circumstances. This is so equally in criminal cases, and if the company is to be convicted it must be proved that the (natural) person in question controlled the management of the company: *R* v *Andrews Weatherfoil Ltd* (1972). A difficulty arises here where a sole director is charged with conspiring with the company: conspiracy necessarily requires two independent minds, and these cannot be found if it is established that the company has no mind or intelligence independent of the will of the sole director: *R* v *McDonnell* (1965).

In *R* v *ICR Haulage* (1944) it was held that the company could be criminally liable for the wrongful act of its managing director even though the act was outside the normal ambit of his duties. *Lennard's Carrying Co* v *Asiatic Petroleum* suggests that the position would be the same in tort.

The second area of difficulty concerns the liability of a company for torts and crimes committed by its officers and employees in the course of ultra vires activities. As a matter of strict logic it may be suggested that it can never be within the course of employment to do ultra vires acts, but this argument seems to prove too much - it might equally be argued that the commission of a tort or crime must always be ultra vires. It is suggested that a court would not accept this argument, though in logic it is hard to see how it can be rebutted.

It may be noted finally that one effect of the 'alter ego' doctrine is to circumvent the problem of imposing liability for offences which require a specific intent; even if the company cannot form the intent, its alter ego presumably can, and this is enough to found liability.

HLT GROUP PUBLICATIONS FOR THE LLB EXAMINATIONS

Our publications, written by specialists, are used widely by students at universities, polytechnics and colleges throughout the United Kingdom and overseas.

Textbooks

These are designed as working books to provide students with a valuable framework on which to base their studies. They are updated each year to reflect new developments and changing trends.

Casebooks

These are designed as companion volumes to the Textbooks and incorporate important cases, statutes as appropriate, and other material, together with detailed commentaries.

Revision WorkBooks

For first degree law students, these provide questions and answers for all topics in each law subject. Every topic has sections on key points, recent cases and statutes, further reading etc.

Suggested Solutions

These are available to past London University LLB examination papers and provide the student with an invaluable revision aid and an insight into the techniques essential to examination success.

The books listed below can be ordered through your local bookshops or obtained direct from the publisher using this order form. Telephone, Fax or Telex orders will also be accepted. Quote your Access or Visa card numbers for priority orders. To order direct from the publisher please enter the cost of the titles you require, fill in the despatch details and send it with your remittance to the HLT Group Ltd.

ORDER FORM

LLB PUBLICATIONS	Textbooks Cost £	£	Casebooks Cost £	£	Revision WorkBooks Cost £	£	Sug. Sol. 1984/88 Cost £	£	Sug. Sol. 1989 Cost £	£
L01 Criminal Law	12.95		16.95		9.95		14.95		3.95	
L02 Constitutional Law	12.95		16.95		9.95		14.95		3.95	
L03 English Legal System	12.95		14.95				*6.95		3.95	
L04 Law of Contract	12.95		15.95		9.95		14.95		3.95	
L05 Law of Tort	12.95		16.95				14.95		3.95	
L06 Law of Trusts	12.95		16.95		9.95		14.95		3.95	
L07 Land Law	12.95		18.95		9.95		14.95		3.95	
L08 Jurisprudence	14.95				9.95		14.95		3.95	
L09 Administrative Law	15.95		18.95				14.95		3.95	
L10 Law of Evidence	17.95		14.95		9.95		14.95		3.95	
L11 Commercial Law	17.95		18.95		9.95		14.95		3.95	
L13 Pub. Int. Law	16.95		14.95		9.95		14.95		3.95	
L14 Succession	14.95		15.95		9.95		14.95		3.95	
L16 Family Law	14.95		18.95				14.95		3.95	
L17 Company Law	16.95		18.95		9.95		14.95		3.95	
L18 Revenue Law	14.95		18.95		9.95		14.95		3.95	
L20 European Community Law	15.95									

Cut along dashed line

* 1987 and 1988 only

DETAILS FOR DESPATCH OF PUBLICATIONS
Please insert your full name below

Please insert below the style in which you would like correspondence to be addressed to you

TITLE Mr, Miss etc.	INITIALS	SURNAME/FAMILY NAME

Address to which study material is to be sent (please ensure someone will be present to accept delivery of your College Publications.)

POSTAGE & PACKING
You are welcome to purchase study material from the College at 200 Greyhound Road W14 9RY, during normal working hours.

If you wish to order by post this may be done direct from the College. Postal charges are as follows:

UK   - all orders over £25 - no charge; orders below £25 - £1.50.
OVERSEAS   - all orders are sent by airmail and the charge is £6 for the first item, an additional £4 for the second item and an additional £3 for the third and for every additional item. If ordering *Suggested Solutions 1989 only* add 30% to the charge for the Suggested Solutions ordered.

The College cannot accept responsibility in respect of postal delays or losses in the postal systems.

DESPATCH All cheques must be cleared before material is despatched.

SUMMARY OF ORDER

Date of order: [/   /   ]

Cost of publications ordered: £ [   ]
Add: Postage and packing United Kingdom (see above)   £ [   ]
Overseas Air Mail: First item at £6; Second item at £4;
 Additional items at £3; Suggested Solutions only: 30%

Total cost of order: £ [   ]

Please ensure that you enclose a cheque or draft payable to The HLT Group Ltd for the above amount, or charge to   ☐ Access   ☐ Visa

Card Number [| | | | | | | | | | | | | | |]

Expiry Date [/   /   ]   Signature _____

Your completed form and remittance should be sent to :
The HLT Group Ltd, Despatch Department, 200 Greyhound Road, London W14 9RY.
Telephone: (01) 385 3377 Telex: 266386 Fax: (01) 381 3377.